STRATFORD EAST

Presented by Stratford East

Now, I See

by Lanre Malaolu

Now, I See was first performed at
Stratford East on Friday 10 May 2024

Newham London

Supported using public funding by ARTS COUNCIL ENGLAND

REG. NO 556251 | VAT NO 233 3120 59 | CHARITY REG. NO 233801

CAST

KIERON	Oliver Alvin-Wilson
DAYO	Nnabiko Ejimofor
ADEYEYE	Tendai Humphrey Sitima

CREATIVE TEAM

Writer, Director, Movement Director	Lanre Malaolu
Scenographer	Ingrid Hu
Costume Designer	Debbie Duru
Lighting Designer	Ryan Day
Composer	Jan Brzezinski
Sound Designer	Pär Carlsson
Associate Director	Kirk-Ann Roberts
Assistant Choreographer	Rochea Dyer
Production Dramaturg	Roy Alexander Weise
Dramaturg	Anthony Simpson-Pike
Production Dramatherapist	Wabriya King
Costume Supervisor	Olivia Ward
Artist Collaboration	Joseph Ijoyemi
Tailor for Dayo's Costume	Mario Thompson

PRODUCTION TEAM

Production Manager	Daniel Steward
Head of Production	Phil Connolly
Stage Manager on the Book	Meghan Hodgson
Head of Stage	Jez Ward
Head of Sound	Joe Killen
Company Stage Manager	Vanessa Sutherland
Lighting Deputy	Bram Walkling-Lea
Lighting Programmer	Paul Birks
Technician	Marc Thornton
Wardrobe Manager	Liv Koplick
Production Assistant	Kezia Beament
Producer	Sean Brooks
Senior Producer	Catherine Morgenstern
Trailer filming	Monika Davies
Photography	Camilla Greenwell

FEATURED SONGS

'Ye' – Burna Boy
'Superstar' – Usher
'Spirit 2.0' – Sampha
'Sampha's Plea' – Stormzy
'Give It to the Water' – Stormzy

BIOGRAPHIES

OLIVER ALVIN-WILSON | KIERON

Theatre credits include: *Disruption* (Park Theatre); *All Of Us* (National Theatre); *Henry VI Rebellion / The War of The Roses* (Royal Shakespeare Company); *Samskara* (Yard Theatre); *The Doctor* (Almeida); *The Twilight Zone* (Almeida/Ambassadors Theatre); *Nine Night* (National Theatre/Trafalgar Studios); *Genesis Inc.* (Hampstead Theatre); *Hamlet* (HamletScenen); *A Midsummer Night's Dream* (Young Vic); *The Red Barn, Emperor and Galilean, All's Well That Ends Well* (National Theatre); *Othello* (Stafford Gatehouse); *A Midsummer Night's Dream, The Merchant of Venice, Henry V* (Propellor Theatre Company); *Antigone* (Stratford East/Pilot Theatre); *Doctor Faustus* (Leeds Playhouse/Citizen's Theatre); *Blue/Orange* (National Tour); *Romeo and Juliet, This Child* (Pilot Theatre); *Antony and Cleopatra* (Nuffield Theatre); *To Kill a Mockingbird* (Theatre Clwyd/Tour); *Pigeon Love* (The Space); *Much Ado About Nothing* (Derby Live); *The Gala, World Poetry Day Recital, Seven Ages of Poetry* (RSC).

Film/short film includes: *Harkness, Wonder Woman 1984, The Huntsman, Kerry, River Cross, Karmic Compensation, The Fields, Interview for Life, Dead End.*

Television credits include: *Curfew, The Lord of the Rings: Rings of Power, The Bay, Murder in Provence, The Rebel, Collateral, Lovesick, From Cradle to Grave, Misfits, Hollyoaks, Casualty.*

NNABIKO EJIMOFOR | DAYO

Nnabiko trained at RADA.

Theatre credits include: *Jitney* (The Old Vic/Headlong); *For Black Boys Who Have Considered Suicide When The Hue Gets Too Heavy* (The Royal Court Theatre / New Diorama / Apollo Theatre – Olivier Award nomination for Best Supporting Actor and winner of the 2022 Stage Debut Award Best Performer in a Play).

Short film includes: *Good Vibes Only, Figure.*

TENDAI HUMPHREY SITIMA | ADEYEYE

Tendai trained at RADA.

Theatre credits include: *A Strange Loop* (Trafalgar Theatre Productions & National Theatre); *The Play That Goes Wrong* (Kenny Wax Productions); *Malindadzimu* (Hampstead Theatre); *Hoarding* (Sheep Soup); *Immersive Great Gatsby* (Immersive Everywhere); *The Tales Of Beatrix Potter* (Gobbledigook); *Neverland* (Guild of Misrule); *Titus Andronicus* (Time Zone Theatre).

TV credits include: *The Winter Palace* (Netflix); *Doghouse* (Made Television Network & Mr. Left Productions).

Alongside his professional credits, Tendai is also an accomplished recording artist, multi-instrumentalist, and composer.

LANRE MALAOLU | Writer, Director, Movement Director

Lanre is an award-winning writer, director, and choreographer known for his groundbreaking fusion of movement and dialogue to tell socially engaged stories. His stage production *SAMSKARA* received critical acclaim and was published by Nick Hern Books.

Lanre's films have gained international acclaim. His short film *The Circle* was acquired by The Guardian having screened globally, including a world premiere at Sheffield Doc/Fest. *The Conversation* earned him the Best Director award at the Soul Film Festival and Best Dance Film at the Aesthetica Film Festival. He is currently developing his first feature with BBC FILM.

INGRID HU | Scenographer

Ingrid Hu is a scenographer, designer and artist. She received her MA in Scenography from Central St Martins in London and has been working in theatre and multidisciplinary design over the past 20 years. With a focus on materiality, contextual and conceptual thinking, she creates spaces and environments that are alive and empowered to co-author and respond to contemporary narratives.

She joined the award-winning Heatherwick Studio in 2002 and has worked on a wide range of projects including the UK Pavilion for the 2010 World Expo, for which she received a D&AD award in Spatial Design.

Recent theatre credits include: *Something in the Air* (Schauspielhaus Bochum, Germany); *Turandot* (Arcola Theatre, UK); *Song from Far Away* (HOME Manchester & Hampstead Theatre, UK); *We Need New Names* (Brixton House, UK Tour); *In The Net* (Jermyn Street Theatre); *No Particular Order* (Theatre 503); *The Global Playground* (Manchester Int'l Festival & Theatre Rites); *Mission* (The Big House); *Chotto Xenos* (Akram Khan, World Tour); *Athena* And *A Kettle Of Fish* (The Yard Theatre, London); *A Slightly Annoying Elephant* (Little Angel Theatre, London); *Light/Dark* (Uppsala, Sweden); *Curiouser* (UK/Norway Tour); *Zeraffa Giraffa* (Little Angel Theatre And Clapham Omnibus Theatre, London); *We Raise Our Hands In The Sanctuary* (The Albany, London); *Hong Kong Impressions* (Yuen Long Theatre, Hong Kong); *1908 Body And Soul* (Jacksons Lane Theatre, London); And *You May!* (The Place, Arnolfini, UK; Onassis Culture Centre, Greece).

DEBBIE DURU | Costume Designer

Debbie Duru is a designer for performance spaces.

Theatre credits as Set & Costume designer include *Beneatha's Place* (Young Vic); *Run Rebel* (Pilot Theatre/Mercury Theatre); *Ravenscourt* (Hampstead Theatre); *The White Card* (Northern Stage); *Two Billion Beats* (Orange Tree Theatre); *The Song Project* (Royal Court); *...cake* (Theatre Peckham); *Dagny Wants to Dance* (Bureau of Silly Ideas); *Josephine* (Theatre Royal Bath).

Theatre credits as Costume designer include *Twice Born* (Scottish Ballet/Theatre Royal Glasgow); *Romeo and Juliet* (Almeida); and *Alice in Wonderland* (Brixton House).

Credits as Associate Set designer include *Mandela, The Musical* (Young Vic); *Get Up Stand Up! The Bob Marley Musical* (Lyric Theatre) and *Dick Whittington* (National Theatre).

She is the winner of the Black British Theatre Award 2023 for Theatre design, recipient of an Offie Nomination as Costume designer for *Alice in Wonderland*, and was a Linbury Prize finalist 2019.

RYAN DAY | Lighting Designer

Ryan is a lighting designer for theatre, dance, opera, and fashion. Ryan enjoys working in close collaboration with the creative team, introducing and maintaining positive working relationships.

He studied Theatre Lighting Design at The Royal Central School of Speech and Drama.

Theatre credits include: *The Lion Inside, The Boy at the Back of the Class* (Rose Theatre & UK Tour); *Backstairs Billy* (Duke of York's); *Quiz* (Chichester Festival Theatre & UK Tour); *Never Have I Ever* (Minerva Theatre, Chichester); *Saving Face* (Curve Leicester & The Place); *War and Culture* (New Diorama); *Black Superhero* (Jerwood Theatre Downstairs, Royal Court); *Local Hero* (Co-Lighting Designer, Minerva Theatre, Chichester); *Wild Onion* (Norwich Theatre Royal & UK Tour); *Lizard Boy* (Hope Mill & Edinburgh Fringe); *Mission, The Ballad of Corona V* (The Big House); *Christie Done It, Dr Faustess* (Cockpit Theatre); *Rabbit Hole, Darknet* (Union Theatre); *I Know I Know I Know* (Southwark Playhouse); *Into the Woods, A Merchant of Venice* (Playground Theatre).

As associate/assistant, theatre credits include: *The Rite of Spring* (Sadler's Wells & UK Tour); *Wickies* (Park 200); *The Lemon Table* (Salisbury Playhouse/UK Tour); *Les Misérables, Les Misérables In Concert* (Sondheim).

JAN BRZEZINSKI | Composer

Jan Brzezinski is a Polish composer and sound designer with a background in jazz. His work stems from an interest in combining live instrumentation with synthetic textures.

Stage credits include: *Elephant In The Room* (2019); *Samskara* (2021); *Roll Model* (2023); *At The Foot Of The Brae* (2023).

Film credits include: *The Circle* (2019); *The Conversation* (2019); *Maradona – The Fall* (2021); *Where I Can See Them* (2023); *Sadlers Wells Young Associates* (2023).

PÄR CARLSSON | Sound Designer

Pär is a sound designer, working across theatre, dance and film. Growing up in rural Sweden, his work often reflects on the relationship between the organic and synthetic, nature and technology. The projects he loves working with offer the listener a space to reflect and see themselves. Using tonality and texture, he believes audio is a powerful language to evoke emotion.

KIRK-ANN ROBERTS | Associate Director

Kirk-Ann is a Caribbean born, London-based writer, director and dramaturg. A Roundhouse Resident Artist alumni, graduate of Tamasha Theatre and Young Vic director programmes, she has worked for the likes of Young Vic, The Yard Theatre, Talawa Theatre, Half-Moon, Apples and Snakes and The Watermill Theatre.

ROCHEA DYER | Assistant Choreographer

Rochea Dyer is an interdisciplinary artist, movement director, choreographer and teacher specialising in the combination of art forms such as movement, physical theatre and spoken word. Rochea's aim is to create performance work that triggers deeper thinking by exploring themes that should not be ignored or overlooked in society. At the heart of her work is the intimacy of that spectator/performer relationship and how that connection enhances performance art to a higher level. She has gone from touring at the Edinburgh Fringe Festival and working in the West End on shows such as *Breaking Convention* and *Into the Hoods* by Kate Prince to working as an assistant choreographer for the award winning actor Regé Jean-Page's music video *Don't Wait*. In addition to short award-winning films such as *The Conversation* by Lanre Malaolu; winning best dance film at BAFTA recognised Aesthetica Film Festival & San Francisco Dance Film Festival 2020. The driving force behind Rochea's passion is the art of making revolutionary work.

ROY ALEXANDER WEISE | Production Dramaturg

Roy is a director, writer, and dramaturg who graduated from Rose Bruford College in 2011 with a BA (Hons) in Theatre Directing.

He was Associate Artist at The Red Room in 2011, the BBC Theatre Fellow at the Bush Theatre and the Lyric Hammersmith in 2013–14 and then spent 18 months as Trainee Director at London's Royal Court Theatre. In 2016, Roy was the 19th recipient of the prestigious JMK award for his critically acclaimed production of Katori Hall's *The Mountaintop*.

Notable productions include: *Nine Night, Master Harold & The Boys, Cat On a Hot Tin Roof, Untitled F*** M*** S**gon Play*.

He was Associate Director at the Donmar Warehouse in 2019, and served as Joint Artistic Director & CEO at the Royal Exchange Theatre from 2019–2023. Roy was awarded an MBE in 2020.

ANTHONY SIMPSON-PIKE | Dramaturg

Anthony Simpson-Pike is a director, dramaturg and writer. He was Deputy Artistic Director at the Yard Theatre, Resident Director at Theatre Peckham and Associate Director at the Gate Theatre.

Recent directorial work includes: *Samuel Takes a Break...* at The Yard Theatre, *Beautiful Thing* at Stratford East, *Grenfell: In the Words of Survivors* at the National Theatre (which transferred to St Ann's Warehouse in New York in April 2024); and, at the Bush, Olivier Award-winning *The P Word* and *Lava* (nominated for Best Director at the Black British Theatre Awards); and *An Octoroon* at the Abbey, Dublin (nominated for Best Production at the Irish Times Theatre Awards).

Recent dramaturgical credits include: *Much Ado About Nothing* for the RSC, *Samskara* at the Yard Theatre, *Hotline* with Produced Moon at the Tron, *Dear Young Monster* by Pete McHale for The Queer House, and *Coup de Grace* at the Royal Court.

WABRIYA KING | Production Dramatherapist

Wabriya King is a qualified Dramatherapist (Roehampton University), Actress (Oxford School of Drama), creative facilitator and Reiki practitioner. Wabriya combines her experience to support creatives alongside the rehearsal and performance period.

Dramatherapy support credits include: *Beautiful Thing, Tambo & Bones* (Stratford East); *A Strange Loop* (Barbican Centre); *Cowbois, Falkland Sound, The Empress, Julius Caesar* (RSC); *School Girls, Or, The African Mean Girls Play* (Lyric Hammersmith); *Matthew Bourne's*

Romeo & Juliet (New Adventures); *Drive Your Plow Over the Bones of the Dead* (Complicité); *Romeo & Juliet, Secret Life of Bees* (The Almeida); *August In England* (Bush Theatre); *For Black Boys Who Have Considered Suicide When The Hue Gets Too Heavy* (New Diorama Theatre/Royal Court/West End); *Blue* (ENO); *Further than the Furthest Thing* (Young Vic); *Family Tree* (Actors Touring Company); *Bootycandy* (Gate Theatre); *Blues for an Alabama Sky* (National Theatre); *Hamilton, Moulin Rouge* (West End); *Shifters* (Bush Theatre); *Samuel Takes A Break...* (The Yard Theatre).

OLIVIA WARD | Costume Supervisor

Olivia Ward has worked in theatrical costume for the last 12 years including Running Wardrobe on productions such as *Charlie and the Chocolate Factory, Dreamgirls, Old Times, The Audience* and many others. Most recently she has been Head of Costume (maternity cover) at the Young Vic.

Work as Assistant Supervisor includes: *Plenty* at Chichester Festival Theatre and *Hamlet* at the Young Vic.

As Supervisor: Young Company Season and *Daddy* at the Almeida; *The Collaboration, The Second Woman* and *Beneatha's Place* at the Young Vic; *Kabul Goes Pop* at Brixton House Theatre; *We Started to Sing* at the Arcola; and *The Trials* at the Donmar.

As Associate Costume Designer: *Macbeth* for Frankie Bradshaw and Wessex Grove Productions.

JOSEPH IJOYEMI | Artist Collaboration

Based in London, Joseph Ijoyemi is an Afro-Swedish contemporary and co-founder of The Collective Makers – an organisation helping young creatives in his community to expand their practice through mentorship, collaboration and empowerment. Graduating from Central Saint Martins with an MA in Fine Art in 2023, Joseph's exceptional dedication has earned him recognition, including the prestigious Helen Scott Lidgett Award supported by ACME. He was also shortlisted for the Evening Standard Prize 2023, leading to a group exhibition, and being selected to showcase his work at the esteemed New Contemporaries 2023, solidifying his position as an emerging artist. Collaborating with institutions such as Royal Museums Greenwich, Peabody, Woolwich Works, and the Royal Borough of Greenwich, Joseph's current practice delves into his Nigerian heritage, focusing on his parents' hometown and its historical and cultural significance. Exploring museums housing Nigerian collections, he uncovers ancestral stories, aiming to illuminate the complexity and richness of Nigerian history. Joseph's art serves as a platform for dialogue, inviting viewers to reflect on restitution, cultural heritage, and identity. Employing diverse mediums, he creates immersive experiences that challenge preconceptions and celebrate the resilience, strength, and beauty of Black communities. Each piece prompts viewers to question norms, delve into untold histories, and embrace cultural diversity. Committed to sparking conversations and fostering empathy, Joseph's work offers a fresh perspective on the African diaspora, shaping narratives and cultivating connections in contemporary art.

STRATFORD EAST

We are Stratford East. We're here to push boundaries, champion talent and create hard-hitting shows in the beating heart of east London. We're here to move you, excite you and keep theatre open for all.

We have been telling stories since 1884. Many leading actors, writers and directors have been part of the family including Meera Syal, Barbara Windsor, Don Warrington, Indhu Rubasingham, Tanika Gupta, Roy Williams and Cynthia Erivo.

With Artistic Director Nadia Fall at the helm, we present a bold programme of reimagined classics, timely revivals and ground-breaking new work.

SUPPORTERS OF STRATFORD EAST

We would like to thank all of our generous current supporters

MAJOR SUPPORTERS
Barry and Ann Scrutton
Rosalind Riley and Tim Bull
Joan Leith

INDIVIDUAL SUPPORTERS
Andrew Cowan
Dr Elizabeth Glyn
The Daniel and Gaynor Harris Trust
Nicolas Kent
Mark Gorman

LITTLEWOOD CIRCLE MEMBERS
Neil and Sarah Brener
Grand Cru Consulting

CRYSTAL MEMBERS
Matt Clarson
Nigel Farnall and Angelica Puscasu
Patricia Hamzahee
Stephen and Angela Jordan
Elizabeth and Derek Joseph
Rachel Potts for Jon Potts

PEARL MEMBERS
Stephanie Barrows
Susan Fletcher
Mary Friel
Good Wolf People
Patricia Hewitt
Christopher Hird
Andrew Hochhauser QC
Rt Hon Dame Margaret Hodge MP
Melanie J. Johnson
Jean Lang
Derek Paget
Martin Pilgrim MBE
Bryan Raven
Hedy Richards
Andrew Simmonds
Danielle Whitton

HONEY MEMBERS
Tom Adeyoola
Hamida Aziz
Katie Bradford
Steve Bundred
Simon Carruth and Janet Gormley
Anthony Chantry
Fiona Clements
Steve Edge & Jane Fogg
Andrew Grenville
Colin Guthrie
Jonathan Levy
Tracy Pinnock
Heather Rogers
John Stokes
Wendy Thompson
Rob Whiteman

TRUSTS AND FOUNDATIONS
Aspers Good Causes Fund
Bunbury Charitable Trust
Charles S French Charitable Trust
The Childhood Trust
The Fenton Arts Trust
The Garrick Club Charitable Trust
Harold Hyam Wingate Foundation
Idlewild Trust
John Thaw Foundation
Maria Björnson Memorial Fund
National Lottery Community Fund
National Lottery Heritage Foundation
Noël Coward Foundation
Teale Charitable Trust

CORPORATE PARTNERS AND SUPPORTERS
Aloft Hotel Excel
Clarion Futures
Devonshires Solicitors
Good Hotels
Kromanti Rum
Pinsent Masons LLP

And all our Friends of Stratford East as well as those who wish to remain anonymous.

To find out more about how you can support Stratford East, go to **stratfordeast.com/supportus**

FOR STRATFORD EAST

Artistic Director Nadia Fall
Executive Director Eleanor Lang

ARTISTIC
Senior Producer Catherine Morgenstern
Producer Sean Brooks

PRODUCTION
Head of Production Phil Connolly
Lighting Deputy Bram Walkling-Lea
Head of Stage Jez Ward
Head of Sound Joe Killen
Company Stage Manager Vanessa Sutherland
Production Assistant Kezia Beament

ADMINISTRATION
Planning Manager Georgina Easterbrook-Matthews
Administrator and PA to the Artistic Director Josie Griffiths
Executive Assistant & HR Officer Holly Burgess
Live Events & Hires Programmer Martin Willis

OPERATIONS
Operations Director Nichola Ivey
Theatre Operations Manager Jovan Jeremiah
IT Systems Manager Stuart Saunders
Project Manager Barry Cronin
Duty Managers Sophy Johnston, Beatrix Webb, Juan Casanellas, Itoya Osagiede, Valery Reva, Jayro Viapree
Stratford East Trading Manager Nailah Cumberbatch

FINANCE
Finance Director Patrick Holzen
Financial Controller Colleen Francis
Finance Manager Ashley Tsen
Finance Assistant Maryna Orlova

DEVELOPMENT
Development Director Anna Clark
Development Manager Claire Leith

LEARNING & PARTICIPATION
Learning & Participation Director Flo Paul
Community & Participation Producer Kirstin Shirling
Education and Learning Producer Rebecca Goh
Learning & Participation Coordinator Bethan Barke

MARKETING & SALES
Marketing & Communications Director Sarah Clark
Marketing Officer Rhys Williams
140th Programme Producer Emma Jerrold
PR Agency Jo Allan PR
Audience Experience Manager Angela Frost
Box Office Supervisor Asha Bhatti, Amaryllis Courtney
Box Office Assistants Judy Mackenzie, Rosie Revan, Elise Ward-Mollett

FRONT OF HOUSE
Deputy Duty Managers Jade Benjamin, Carlos Byles, Rosie Christian, Rosie Revan, Sophia Towli, Sarah-Jayne Johnson
Front of House Supervisors Emma Cavell King, Shifali Dunbar, Jevani Emmanuel, Elsie Frangou, Sofia Genuise, Isobel Hardcastle, Matthew Malin, Matilda Rae, Jake Rix
Front of House Assistants Fatima Abukar, Alexandra Craviero, Pele Green, Charlotte Mak, Melissa McCabe, Phoebe McDonnell, Skye Mitchell, Abdul Sessay, Sayful Taneem, Zephaniah Tokossi, Elise Ward-Mollett, Georgina Hackett, Caitlin Haste, Aisha Creary, Edward Justham, Kelvin Atmadibrata, Mascuud Dahir, Nevaeh Hamilton-Bolessa, Rhianna Boyce-Barrett, Samuel Tawel, Ethan Lyons, Isaac Ellis, Joshua-Alexander Williams, Khairah Francis-Shayek, Yusuf Shahzad, Cameron Essam, Amaal Blake, Tia Killen

BAR
Assistant Bar Manager Tia Fernandez
Bar Supervisors Tramaiyne Jeremiah, Jayro Viapree, Rebecca Goh, Phoebe Pennington, Dom Elcock, Megan Slater, Shem Glowacki
Bar Assistants Rashaan Anselm, Emma Cavell King, Ariana Xenofontos, Caitlin Haste, Blake Creighton, Georgina Hackett, Holly Demaine, Maya Marsh, Zephaniah Tokossi, Jake Rix, Jianhang Wang, Clara Doherty, Ikesha Patrick, Sarah Carvalho, Isla Mcleod, Nef McHenry

BUILDING & FACILITIES
Building and Facilities Manager Graeme Bright
Building Maintenance Technicians Mackie Francis
Domestic Assistants Vida Osei Bowman, Vincent McGrath, Marjorie Walcott, Sydney Weise

NOW, I SEE

Lanre Malaolu

Move, move, move, become overwhelmed by the water, let it wash over you, let the trauma rise up like vomit, spill it, go on, let it spill on the ground, let go of the pain, let go of the fear, let go. You are safe here…

Open Water*, Caleb Azumah Nelson*

The day the child realizes that all adults are imperfect, he becomes an adolescent; the day he forgives them, he becomes an adult; the day he forgives himself, he becomes wise.

Alden Nowlan

Author's Note

A few thank-yous and shout-outs…

Rachel Taylor and Helena Clark, you are incredible humans and incredible agents. Thank you for giving me feedback on the first draft, and your continued support. Here's to more belly laughs and tinned beans talk.

Laura M, thank you for your gift, a book which profoundly impacted me while writing *Now, I See*.

Beth Turrell, thank you for the sacred space and for believing in me.

Tunmise, it's beautiful that you became my brother-in-law as I was writing a piece about brotherhood. Our chats and your energy gave me momentum during the final stages of its creation.

To Daniel, Nathaniel, AJ and to all my brothers beyond my blood, I See you.

Finally, to every soul in the cast and creative team, you are deeply special. Never forget to S.A.S. if, and when, you need to.

L.M.
2024

Characters

ADEYEYE, *late thirties, Black*
KIERON, *early forties, Black*
DAYO, *early thirties, Black*

These men are brothers.

Notes

A dash (–) is used to indicate an interruption and a slash (/) denotes an overlapping in dialogue.

Words in **bold** within a character's line denote where movement happens, either as the word is *spoken*, or to *replace* the word.

All movement sequences and stage directions are a template. The performers and collaborators will use this as a base to work from. Many ideas may stay, many may go.

I wouldn't call this a play.

I also wouldn't call this a dance show.

This text went to press before the end of rehearsals and so may differ slightly from the play as performed.

Prologue

As the audience takes their seats, there will be a subtle underscore of hushed sounds of the sea, as…

ADEYEYE *bounces in front of a gauze on the stage. He shoots into a boxing stance every now and then, throws a few jabs, slips, rolls… and again. This continues until our audience are all seated, then…*

LIGHTS UP.

ADEYEYE *bursts into a physical journey of boxing. His body full of joy and unbounded autonomy… JAB – JAB – JAB – SLIP – he's loving it… SLIP – SLIP – SLIP – ROLL – a portrait of a man in flow… more jabs – more slips – more smiles – but then, subtle hints of pain slip into his body. He tries to ignore it, but they get louder and louder. He stops, confused. Beat. Then takes a deep breath in… and… exhales… in… and…*

On his next exhale, the gauze rises, to reveal a casket. Its walls are see-through. It's full to the brim, with water.

ADEYEYE *looks meaningfully at the casket, his body filling with an ethereal energy. He takes a deep breath in, closes his eyes and begins to hum 'Amazing Grace' – not a passionate rendition, but a calling… an invitation. Eyes open, he searches the space. Beat. The humming continues, with even more intent. Then…*

DAYO *enters, dressed in Nigerian attire; his eyes are locked on the casket. He doesn't acknowledge* ADEYEYE. *It's as if they are in two different spaces, yet still connected.* DAYO *steps towards the casket, his approach soft yet inquisitive – apprehensive, but drawn to it.* ADEYEYE*'s eyes soften momentarily before scanning the space again, as if someone is missing. His humming intensifies, as he strains to summon someone else.*

Eventually, KIERON *enters in a suit, body heavy, eyes lost. Like* DAYO*, he doesn't acknowledge* ADEYEYE. *Glancing* *between* DAYO *and the casket, confused yet intrigued,* KIERON *takes a step closer… then stops. A chasm of space between him and the casket. Between him and* DAYO.

ADEYEYE *steps back, eyes locked on them both. His hum now feels like a plea.* KIERON *looks up at* DAYO, *then back at the casket's waters. A palpable tension in his body builds and, after a beat, he bolts offstage.*

DAYO*'s gaze returns to the casket then, after a beat, he saunters offstage, leaving…*

ADEYEYE (*singing*).

…I once was lost, but now I'm found was blind but… I once was lost, but now I'm found, was blind but… but…

He can't finish the song. He can't find the words, or the words can't find him. Beat. He takes a deep breath in and –

BLACKOUT.

In darkness, he continues to breathe…

In… and –

Exhale…

In… and –

On his final exhale, muffled sounds of the sea merge with his breath and eventually become the only sounds we hear…

The waves sweep the theatre, wash the walls, swish under our feet, run towards us –

Closer…

Closer…

The waves are about to wash right over us…

And –

SOUND OFF – LIGHTS UP.

ACT ONE

The space is now filled with a table, chairs and a broom, scattered around – a disused storage room. Muffled sounds of Nigerian music thump outside the room, along with laughter and chatter from people.

ADEYEYE *is no longer in the space, but will appear and disappear sporadically as the piece progresses.*

The door opens, a wave of music and lights floods the room. KIERON *strolls in, clutching a bottle of water. He swiftly shuts the door and lets out a long, relieved breath, as though he's been quietly enduring something. He looks around the room, unimpressed. Starts to move things around… table to the corner, tucks chairs in, etc. Goes over to the broom and sweeps, frantically. Nods his head, this will do. Grabs a chair, wipes the seat several times, then sits. Beat.*

He takes a swig of water, then gazes at the bottle. After a moment, he slowly pours a bit of it onto the floor, a libation. This moment activates lights that gently rise on ADEYEYE *and the casket.*

KIERON *tries to look towards them, but struggles… a palpable tension within. After a beat, he jumps up; lights on the casket fade. He looks at the water on the floor, then around the space… grunts, no sign of what he's looking for. Exits upstage-right into a closet, shuffles in it.*

DAYO *enters with a plastic plate full of chicken, and a small wooden box.* DAYO *looks around, baffled, looks towards the closet.*

DAYO. Kieron?… You good?

> *Beat.* DAYO *glances at the wooden box, then quickly conceals it in a corner. Eats.*

> You tried this chicken yet?!… CERTIFIED!!… Nah, yeah, nah this, along with the jollof is top priority for the

Tupperware… talking of Tupperware, can you believe I saw some aunties circling the table with theirs already!…

At least give it a couple hours, man, jeeez!! And you know what the maddest thing is?!… I ain't seen half these aunties before in my life!! Like, where do they…?! I swear, there must be some kind of sorority where aunties from all walks of life, meet up for weekly coffees, while they make maps of random people's weddings, parties… roll in, like they know everyone, blatantly fill up their ten containers and dust on to the next! Scavengers!

KIERON *re-enters, doesn't connect eyes with* DAYO. *Goes directly to the chair and sits.*

KIERON (*to himself*). A towel, a broom, a flippin yoga mat and no…?!

DAYO. No…?

Beat. DAYO *glances at the water on the floor.*

There's water on the floor by the way. (*Beat.*) You good?…

Beat. DAYO *runs over to the door opens it slightly.*

Yo, you gotta check this!… He's sat across from the DJ…

No response from KIERON. DAYO *closes it.*

There's always one!… One uncle sat with his swollen belly and dry ankles, eyeing up all the girls less than half his age! And the messed-up thing is he's probably related to half of them!! (*Beat.*) Ain't seen you on the dance floor yet!… You'd probably still whoop my ass at sprinting, but trust me, my foot shuffle has reached super / sayin –

KIERON. Look, I just came in here for some… so… you know.

DAYO.…Piss off?

KIERON. Your words, not mine, but… you know.

DAYO. Cool. I'll finish this drumstick off and… you know. (*Beat.*) Been attacked by Aunty Funke yet? I'm a grown-ass man and she's still there squeezing my cheeks like I'm five! But I don't do anything! It's crazy how you automatically morph back into a child when with certain family.

KIERON. Woman ain't looked at me once.

Beat.

DAYO. You eaten?

KIERON. Am I ten?

DAYO. It's just… I've seen you slip in and out of the hall like three, four times like you're doing something, going somewhere… I wanted to make sure you're okay / and –

KIERON *sighs, loud and heavy.*

Even at the church… I'm sure the pastor appreciated you packing up the whole hall and sweeping every corner of the floor after the / service –

KIERON. And?

DAYO. Nah, I'm not… it's good, it was… Just… feels like maybe you've been –

KIERON *shoots up.*

Where you going?

KIERON. Mop.

DAYO. I'll get it.

KIERON. Nah, it's…

DAYO. I'll get it.

KIERON *continues, gets to the door, but stops as –*

I don't care. About what happened… I want you to know that I don't care.

This affects KIERON, *yet he does his best to hide it – he exits.* DAYO *goes over to the bottle of water. Looks at it, then pours some in the exact same spot* KIERON *did. A libation. Lights rise on* ADEYEYE *and the casket.*

The moment I found out… the first thing that came to my mind was Uber Eats. Two whole months of free food! We could have run the hustle for years! Until the whole hood started doing it and they clocked on. We had a decent run though… Those Saturday afternoons…

Sounds of ocean waves sweep us into the following moment, a memory. ADEYEYE *floats into the space, 'Ye' by Burna Boy underscores the scene as if played through portable speakers.*

Doing our walk round Vikki Park, then chilling on a bench, merking Uber Eats, Burna Boy blaring on your speakers and just… doing a whole load of nothing. Chilling, talking, watching stupid YouTube videos. (*Beat.*) It's crazy how a whole load of nothing, suddenly becomes everything. (*Beat.*) The amber-green colour of the leaves… the angle of sun, the uneven concrete, the Indian bruddas playing cricket in the field, the birdshit on the bench we'd cover up with the amber-green leaves, the endless flow of middle-aged white women jogging past… I just don't get where they all come from?!… Ahhh the way the food sat in my belly! That Cajan chicken burger, extra jalapeños, sweet potato fries, buffalo wings, a Fanta Fruit Twist and… your face. (*Beat.*) The way you'd close your eyes with deep passion, like you were French-kissing the love of your life with every bite of that, veggie cheeseburger, extra cheese, no pickles… DEAD, but, you loved it.

The way you'd purposely let a line of mayo chill on your top lip and never wiped it, 'cause you knew it annoyed the hell out of me. How whenever I said Red Nose Day, you'd…

ADEYEYE *gently wipes his nose.*

'Cause your nose always used to sweat when you eat. (*Beat.*) All those nothings. (*Beat.*) No one teaches you about this, you know? Not just how to deal with it, but how to deal with yourself in it, find yourself in it… Have I actually ever found myself? Feel like I've spent a bulk of my life bouncing from thing to thing, from you, to work, home, to hospital and now that the bouncing's stopped, just feel like I'm **floating**. Maybe I always have been. It's hard to know 'cause I've never looked down to see where my feet were at until now. How do I stop **floating**?…

Through a series of movements, ADEYEYE *tries to pull* DAYO *down as his body floats up – this all happens without physical contact – but he fails.* ADEYEYE *then starts towards the casket, dips his hands in, then offers the water to* DAYO. DAYO *looks at the offered hands, a flicker of longing, but a force holds him back, when –*

Ocean waves swell into the space. KIERON *shoots in, expressively circles the space with a mop, comes to the feet of* ADEYEYE, *but doesn't look up to him, instead trucks on…*

Lights change – back to the room. KIERON *mops.*

KIERON. I travelled from Hertfordshire to Hackney for some soggy chips and dry-ass chicken. I remember.

DAYO. All you remember was the Nando's?

KIERON. It was a traumatic meal.

DAYO. We didn't talk that much to be fair. Looked like you couldn't wait to leave.

KIERON. 'Cause my belly was backflipping!

DAYO. You know those friends you don't see for years, but as soon as you sit down, chop it up, feels like it was yesterday? (*Beat.*) I remember sipping my water in silence thinking, I'm sat across from my blood, but feels like –

KIERON. I talked more than you did! You hardly said a word.

DAYO. 'Cause any time I mentioned his name / you'd –

KIERON. About you. Hardly said a word about you.

DAYO. You doing that didn't really make me wanna speak about… there were things he wanted me to… things *I* wanted / to –

KIERON. Be your own man. Anyway, that was five years ago. Forward.

DAYO *shifts. Takes a bite of food. A long beat. Music blares from outside.*

Where you find this DJ?! Facebook Marketplace?! I keep telling him not to play the music so loud!! Watch him blow something!

Beat.

DAYO. How's work?

KIERON. Same shit, different day.

Beat.

DAYO. Oh, me? Yeah, work's good, man! Just doing some warehouse stuff for Amazon at the moment, but as soon as I get home, I'm bang on my trading. I remember telling him by the time I hit thirty-five I wanna be done working for other people.

KIERON. Gotta step up now.

DAYO. I guess.

KIERON. No guessing, just action.

DAYO *laughs.*

What's funny?

DAYO. *No guessing, just action… Life ain't supposed to be easy!…* Your go-to bars ain't / changed one –

KIERON. Bars?

DAYO. Yeah, you always / used to –

KIERON. Can't lounge your life away, hoping for the best!

DAYO. Come on, I was / only –

KIERON. Gotta move with intention, in every moment, with every choice, otherwise you start lagging and that's when things starts to… bars ya na. It's cool, always thought different to you lot anyway. Just keep your head down, stay focused and always remember why you're doing what you do… Hold on to that, tight.

DAYO. *If you try to change it, you will ruin it… try to hold on to it, you will lose it…* Lao Tzu… Something I read.

KIERON. The way you clung on to that dictionary… hearing you in Mum's room every day, tryna win her over with new words you learned.

DAYO. Win her over?

KIERON. Tryna impress her and that! Anyway, I'm actually reading a lot these days, probably more than you!

DAYO. Swear? What you read?

KIERON. Off the top of my head… *48 Laws of Power*, *12 Rules for Life*, *Never Split the Difference*… That David Goggins book… *Can't… Can't… Hurt Me*! *Can't Hurt Me*… guy's a G! What else… (*Gets phone out, scrolls.*) *Bigger, Leaner, Stronger*…

DAYO. Rah, you've racked them up! How do you find the time?!

KIERON. You don't find it, you make it!

DAYO. I guess, but it's hard with work and was even harder when he was… when he got worse –

KIERON. If anything, just speed them up innit! One-point-five, or two, if you can hack it!

DAYO. …Ohhhhhhhhhh!

KIERON. What?

DAYO. All those titles you mentioned… They're audiobooks.

KIERON. And?

DAYO. They're… audiobooks.

KIERON. You're repeating yourself.

DAYO. It's not really reading, is it?

KIERON. Sorry?

DAYO. Listening to words is not the same as holding a physical book and… Wait, are you…?! You gotta feel the book in your hands, be present with it, allow the words / to –

KIERON. You gotta finish it! Get the words in as fast as you can, move on to the next!

DAYO. That's not reading!

KIERON. Listen, some advice for your next drumstick: big, slow, chews… ideally, thirty-two times.

DAYO. You are not / serious!

KIERON. Real talk! I read that digestion issues can affect brain cognition.

DAYO. Did you *read* that, orrrr… was that a free credit on Audible?

KIERON *lets out a small chuckle. Beat. He takes his jacket off.* DAYO *shoots up, approaches him… puts his hand out. A beat, then,* KIERON *hands it over.* DAYO *hangs it up, then grabs the box.*

He wanted me to give you this.

KIERON. What is it?

DAYO *shrugs.*

Just…

He motions towards the table. DAYO*, with reluctance, places the box on it. Beat. He hurries to the door, opens it and scans. Spotting it, he smiles.*

DAYO. Okay… come, come…

KIERON *looks over at* DAYO*, nonplussed.*

Trust me, you're gonna wanna see this…

KIERON *slowly strolls over, doesn't go too close to* DAYO*, or the door.*

KIERON. What am I looking at?

DAYO. Back table, to the left…

KIERON. …Jeeesus.

DAYO. Right?!

KIERON. Am I missing something?!

DAYO. Remember the last time we saw them like that?! Just… talking, back in the day was more like a musical of slamming doors, flying plates, high-pitched screams…

DAYO *closes the door.* KIERON *saunters off.*

KIERON. From Dad, more than Mum.

DAYO. Eyes bulging out the skull and, of course, the obligatory finger / point.

KIERON. Obliga-what?

DAYO. It means something that they'd always do, whenever / they –

KIERON. Why didn't you just say that? Always used to put your fingers in your ears, chomping down on any food you could get your hands on whenever they argued.

DAYO. Did I?… I can't lie, hated it.

KIERON. People argue, don't get along. It's life.

DAYO. Remember that day they were arguing while we were watching our favourite show?

KIERON. *Your* favourite show.

DAYO. *Mine?* Nah, man, / that was –

KIERON. She bowls into the living room, mid-argument, grabs the fish fingers from your plate, starts flinging them at him at the door!…

DAYO. Then bowls back out…

KIERON. More shouting…

DAYO. Shuffles back in –

KIERON. Cheeks puffed…

DAYO. Eyes full of tears –

KIERON. And is like…

DAYO *and* KIERON. DON'T THROW FOOD AT PEOPLE IN SCHOOL, IT'S NOT GOOD!!

DAYO laughs. KIERON lets one out too, but immediately catches himself. A long beat.

DAYO. The days when I couldn't take the arguing, you'd come over. If I was crying or… You'd come over and hold me / and that would –

KIERON. To stop your high-pitched whining! I came over to make you stop that whining of yours! (*Beat.*) She good though, yeah?… Mum. Saw you with her a lot today.

DAYO. Oh, yeah… she's holding up. She hasn't come talk to / you?

KIERON. Nah, yeah, we said hello and that, but, obviously, you know, there's a lot going on, so…

KIERON *starts off with the mop.*

DAYO. *Our* favourite show.

ADEYEYE *sprints to the door, then performs a Power Ranger move in slow motion.* KIERON *stops, but doesn't acknowledge him.*

KIERON. Huh?

DAYO. It wasn't just mine…

The sound of ocean waves rises and transforms into the Power Rangers *theme song.* DAYO, KIERON *and* ADEYEYE *spring into action, positioning themselves:* KIERON, *centre,* DAYO *to the right,* ADEYEYE *to the left.*

KIERON. IT'S MORPHING TIME!!!

ADEYEYE (*does morphing movement*). Dragon sword!!

KIERON (*does morphing movement*). *Mastodon!!*

DAYO *(does morphing movement*). *Sabretooth tiger!!*

They do a collective 'morphing' movement.

KIERON *glances over at* ADEYEYE *and stops.*

KIERON. Oh my dayyyys, I told you, your hand needs to be out fully otherwise / we won't –

ADEYEYE. It is, man! / I am!

DAYO. Just leave him! I wanna morph, man, I wanna morph!!

KIERON. When Lord Zed eats up your head and spits you out, don't come crying to me!!

He turns back, prepares and –

IT'S MORPHING TIME!!!

ADEYEYE (*does a morphing movement*). Dragon sword!!

KIERON (*does a morphing movement*). *Mastodon!!*

DAYO (*does a morphing movement*). *Sabretooth tiger!!*

The theme song swells as the men spill into the space and fight invisible baddies. The fluorescent lights in the room drop all the way down, and the men remove them, using them as makeshift swords. After a few beats, they regroup. KIERON *gestures at* ADEYEYE *as if saying: 'You're the baddie now.'* ADEYEYE *separates and makes himself look like the baddest baddie he can, then charges over and they continue to play-fight… Until…* ADEYEYE *is accidently hit in the face by* KIERON. *He freezes. The music abruptly stops. Then,* ADEYEYE *starts to cry, but not a 'normal' cry, NOPE… that mouth-wide-open, deep-wail, guttural, ugly kid cry.* KIERON *rolls his eyes, steps away.* DAYO *runs over.*

It's okay, it's okay, you're strong, man, you're / strong!…

KIERON (*kisses teeth*). POWER RANGERS DON'T CRY!!

Lights shift. DAYO *submerges into the depths of the stage.* ADEYEYE *goes back to the casket.* KIERON*'s eyes and body look softer, more willing.*

The previous memory opened something within him… something small, yet an opening.

He approaches the bottle of water, opens it, and begins to pour it out for a libation, but pauses before any drops out. His eyes linger on the bottle for a beat and, instead, he closes his eyes and drinks meaningfully. This action triggers lights to rise on ADEYEYE *and the casket.*

The moment I found out… I was… in my garden. Christine has these birdseed pellets, four of them dotted round each corner. I know what you're thinking… how the hell did I turn into a brudda that has hanging birdseed pellets in his rhatid garden? It was either that, or, two cats… so I said, babygirl, go buy as many pellets as you like! I'm standing there, phone to ear, hearing the words from Dayo's mouth as these flurry of birds sing from theirs. Shooting down and up, down and up, pecking and singing, pecking and singing, couldn't take my eyes off them. And later that night, couldn't take myself to sleep, but when I eventually did, I'm standing in a pitch-black space. And a few metres away from me, is this…

Lights pick up DAYO *as he emerges from the depths of the stage. He is now topless. His body undulates as he approaches.*

…bird. The most beautiful bird I've ever seen…

KIERON *reaches out and tries to physically sculpt the beauty of this bird.* DAYO (*the bird*)*, climbs onto the table, stands on it, and each corner of his body activates with soft and gentle movement.*

Its neck wrapped in thick white feathers, its beak bright red, yellow circles round its blue eyes, feet sharp orange, punctuated with purple stripes – this bird was beautiful! It gazes at me with its soft eyes. I step closer, try to touch it – hold it – I'm stroking it now and as I do, it opens its beak and starts to –

The dulcet tones of strings envelops the space. DAYO*'s movement seamlessly melds with it.*

KIERON*'s body softens further, as he allows the tones to surge through.*

But then… it changes and it starts to… to…

The strings shifts into something harsh. DAYO*'s movement echoes this. It's messy, explosive, unpredictable.*

It's screaming at me! The bird screams at me! I grip it less, must be holding it too tight, but it won't stop! And suddenly, every colour on this bird transforms into black! Jolts out of my hands, hurtles round, circles back to me and I'm running and running! But it catches up to me, makes a beeline to my stomach, flies into it and starts to peck at my innards, starts to strip me down, sinew by sinew, and as it does, it transforms back and forth from the most beautiful bird in the world into this black crow – caged in my chest, cutting at my flesh, fighting to get out – but wants to go deeper! And I'm trying!! Trying to speak the only words that make sense to me, get out – get out – GET OUT! And it does!! And I'm running again, but this time I'm running towards it!! Chasing it screaming the only words that make sense to me, come back – come back – COME BACK!!!

DAYO *submerges back into the depths of the stage.*
A moment.

Can you imagine what that nightmare would have been like if Christine had bought those cats? (*Beat.*) This feeling, this bird… caged in your chest, confused on whether it wants to fly out, or keep chewing, to sing, or scream. Makes you replay everything… What does a man do with all the questions?

ADEYEYE *dips his hands into the casket, goes over to* KIERON *and gently reaches out.* KIERON *doesn't look at or acknowledge* ADEYEYE, *but feels something. There's a small part of him that wants to connect with this moment, with* ADEYEYE*;* KIERON *leans towards him, but a tension still remains.*

(*Shifts.*) No looking back. You wouldn't want that.

Lights fade onto ADEYEYE. *He picks up his boxing stance from the Prologue.*

Moves with joy and autonomy, however, this shifts swiftly as frustration and manic energy consume him; with each failed attempt to command his body through the drills, his rage and fear intensify. The tension builds to a crescendo, when –

KIERON *jolts in, piggybacking* DAYO*: a small insight to their past. They circle the space, then split apart.* KIERON, *downstage-right, engrossed in a video on his phone with the sounds of a sports commentator narrating a race.* DAYO, *upstage-right, looks adrift. A noticeable distance separating them.*

KIERON. Stride, man! Stride!… Legs up and… Jeeesus, don't deserve to be on track with that kind of form, man!…

DAYO *moves centre-stage, a fat grin on his face. He glances towards* KIERON, *clapping his hands loudly before crouching down. He is in position for the game SLAPS.* KIERON *remains absorbed in his video. Undeterred,* DAYO *stays in position and claps his hands again, this time even louder.* KIERON *looks over to him, then back to his phone.* DAYO *does it again.*

You turning into a seal over there or what?

DAYO *releases his position. As he does,* ADEYEYE *stands and moves into the same SLAPS position, then does a slow-motion slap over…*

DAYO. You and Adeyeye…

Ocean waves sweep into the space – ADEYEYE *and* KIERON *jolt centre-stage and begin to play SLAPS in slow motion for a few beats. It's tense.* KIERON *takes a deep breath in as he raises his right hand, about to slap* ADEYEYE, *takes a breath out, and simultaneously, sound of ocean waves sweep us out of the memory.*

KIERON. Always went crying to Mum.

DAYO. 'Cause you always turned it into warfare!

KIERON. I couldn't help that I was faster, stronger!

DAYO. It was just / a game!

KIERON. We made a vow. No matter what happens in the game, never go to Mum. A man's word is his bond.

DAYO. We were teenagers.

KIERON. As soon as your balls drop, you're a man.

Beat. DAYO *goes centre-stage and into the SLAPS position again.* KIERON *doesn't shift.*

DAYO. Let's go! Right now!… Ahh, you're shook innit, I can smell it! Trust me, your reflexes ain't got nuffin on…

No response. DAYO *retreats.*

Yeah, well… guess you gotta look after your health these days.

KIERON *turns to him.*

In the car… I clocked a cheeky grey in your beard…

KIERON. Come here.

DAYO. What?

KIERON. BRING YOUR ASS HERE.

DAYO *strolls over, half-smiling – half-scared.*

Telling a man he's got a grey, is like telling a woman she's put on weight. Even if it's true… YOU DO NOT SAY IT.

DAYO. Yeah, but –

KIERON. Ba!… I look sexy with it anyway…

DAYO. Ermmm…

KIERON. You got some bruddas with them rogue greys, pinging out left, right and centre. No finesse, no style. Don't know how to hold the grey, so, the grey holds them…

DAYO. There's a whole psychology to it?!

KIERON. I can't lie, when the first one popped up last year… September nineteenth, four p.m., to be exact. I might have lost my shit a bit. But now? Can't picture myself without them. Course there's a psychology to it. It's simple… deny it? Makes you ugly; accept it? Sexy. Accept the grey.

DAYO. Accept the grey. I like that. Slyly a metaphor.

KIERON. For what?

DAYO. Life.

KIERON *gazes over at him, grunts. Turns back. Beat. Music from outside blares.*

KIERON. What is this brudda on?!

DAYO. You gonna open it?… The box?

KIERON (*beat*). Suits you.

KIERON *gestures at* DAYO*'s clothes.*

DAYO. Oh… yeah, thanks. I did try to call and text to get your measurements, but / you never –

KIERON. Yeah, nah, my phone's been – been acting up.

DAYO. Doesn't it feel weird seeing the whole family matching and you're –

KIERON. Baa Baa Black Sheep?

DAYO. Huh?

The door opens. Music and lights spill in. KIERON *looks over.*

KIERON. Ayeee, trouble! On a little adventure, yeah!…

KIERON *starts off, exits.*

(*Offstage.*) You eaten?… Okay, go back to Mummy, go on, don't worry we're going soon. Football when we get home, yeah?

KIERON *re-enters. A long beat.*

DAYO. He's got your eyes… and your forehead.

KIERON. Don't let me come over there and…!

DAYO. Why didn't you bring Akin in? (*Beat.*) It was nice to finally meet him today.

KIERON. I sent you pictures.

DAYO. It's a bit different to in person. I can tell he's gonna be a looker though! Gonna break some hearts, just like his pops!…

DAYO*'s words clearly didn't land as he expected.*

I didn't mean… (*Beat.*) How does it feel?… Being a dad?

KIERON. Like everything makes sense, especially when it don't.

DAYO. You thought about how you're gonna give him the talk yet? Just, please… however you do it? Not like Dad.

KIERON *and* DAYO. JUST. USE. PROTECTION.

DAYO (*beat*). What about you?

KIERON. The best defence is offence.

DAYO. Huh?

KIERON. He loves his football, so I'd link it to the game, make sure it sinks in. The best defence, is offence. Always be on the front foot, in football, sex… life. Ain't nothing more important in life, than protecting yourself.

Beat.

DAYO. I'd like to spend time with him… take him out for some food / or go to the –

KIERON. Yeah, yeah, yeah we'll make it happen.

DAYO.…A few weeks?… A month?

KIERON. What's the time?

DAYO. Time?

KIERON. Caretaker said the venue's got back-to-back hires, so gotta make sure the DJ packs up on time. Also, keep an eye on him… dunno what he's on.

KIERON *starts off.* DAYO *shoots centre-stage, and starts to do a physical action – a deadlift.* KIERON *stops.*

DAYO.…Good?

KIERON. What are you…?

DAYO. Yeah, this… this feels good…

KIERON. Terrible.

DAYO. What?!

KIERON. Ab-so-lute-ly / terrible!

DAYO. Feels pretty / good to –

KIERON. Jesus Chr–?!… First and foremost, what on God's earth is your backside doing?! (*Walks over to* DAYO.) Stick that African ass out, man!

DAYO *does.*

And why are your arms so close together…

DAYO. Hip-width apart, no?

KIERON. Shoulders, man! Feet hip-width apart, hands in line with your – ha, you're just tryna piss me off, innit?!

KIERON *goes over to* DAYO, *yanks his body about, during –*

Up! Stand tall. Feet underneath hips… why you looking down for?! Chin up… shoulders lose!!… Okay… down… *slow*… keep that back flat… African ass out… now, on the up… thrust the hips forwards, no swinging… controlled… squeeze the glutes… Let's go… three… two…

They shoot up together as if performing a deadlift, lights slowly change and this seamlessly merges into a brief moment of movement. DAYO*'s body is filled with softness as he gently leans on* KIERON.

This moment holds a profound meaning for him. KIERON, *however, remains stoic and upright throughout it. Beat. He abruptly moves off the spot and to the mop.*

You still got the foundations I taught you somewhere in your body.

DAYO. Got harder to find after you left. Those gym sessions! You'd always push me to go further, lift heavier, followed by the epic Nando's feast we had afterwards! As we bussed jokes / about –

KIERON. You didn't know how to lift, but boy, you knew how to eat!

KIERON *clicks his fingers and gestures to the floor.* DAYO *smiles, quickly assumes the press-up position, with* KIERON *following suit. They start doing press-ups in silence for a beat.* KIERON*'s head is down, and he goes way faster than* DAYO, *who goes at a slower pace, with his head up.*

DAYO. I always used to dream about having shoulders like yours.

DAYO *pauses briefly, not because of fatigue, but to match* KIERON*'s pace, striving for synchronisation.* KIERON *trucks on, but* DAYO *eventually catches the rhythm. They perform press-ups in tandem three times.* KIERON *looks up, clocks, and abruptly rises, appearing uncomfortable. Dusts his hands off.*

KIERON. It's funny, if you told me that back in the day, I would have said hit the gym harder, but…

ADEYEYE *approaches* KIERON. *He slowly reaches out to touch* KIERON*'s shoulders, to hold him, but* KIERON *dips* *and picks up the mop. A disheartened* ADEYEYE *disappears from the space.*

...These shoulders were made outside of it.

Beat. Music from outside blares.

Nahhh this DJ is on crack!!

DAYO. I was seeing this Ghanaian chick.

KIERON (*stops*). Uh-oh.

DAYO. What you got against Ghanaian women?!

KIERON. Nothing! Except for the fact that they still think their jollof is better than ours.

DAYO. Yeah, that's a problem. I asked her what she likes in a man. She said, there's something about a Black man's shoulders. Something she feels drawn to, but won't ever understand.

KIERON. And you?... You a front, or back guy?

DAYO. Rah.

KIERON. We're men here!

DAYO. I... enjoy all sides of a woman.

KIERON. This guy... even now! Always have to say the right things, be the peacekeeper!

DAYO. That a bad thing?

Music from outside starts to rise louder, over –

KIERON. Don't get nowhere in life if you're afraid to cause a fuss! Any time something bad happened, you just shrug it off and smile that smile of yours. Gets to a point, though... Gets a bit disrespectful, you know?

DAYO. Smiling?

KIERON. That's not real life. Can't just smile all the time.

DAYO. There were times you smiled too, times we / all –

KIERON. You and your smiling, him and his singing.

DAYO. Why do you speak like that?

Lights and the music from outside the room suddenly CUT OFF. Complete blackout.

KIERON. THERE YOU GO!! There you…! I done told this brudda! I done…! (*Kisses teeth.*) Flip sake, my phone's dead! Oi, put your torch on…

DAYO (*beat*). Ahhhh, man… my – my phone's dead too…

KIERON. WHAT?!

DAYO. Sorry…

KIERON. Are you / serious?!

DAYO. It's cool! We'll do teamwork! There must be a fusebox in the closet. We'll find it together, it'll be fun!

KIERON. Your idea of fun, is fucked. Now stop playing and put your torch on!

DAYO. You know what this reminds me of, innit?! The *one* game I was good at…

KIERON *walks into something, a loud bang.*

KIERON. Flip sake!

DAYO. It was 'cause of my superhuman hearing! Could hear a pin drop and know exactly where it –

KIERON. Can you just let me focus so I can… (*Hits something.*) Fuuuuck!

DAYO. You always struggled with general bodily awareness. Me on the other hand, coming like Spider-Man!

BANG!… KIERON *hits something else.*

KIERON. JESUS – FLIPPIN – !!!

DAYO. Slow down!

KIERON. THIS IS SO – !?!?

DAYO. Just come to my voice!

A long beat.

KIERON. Say something then!!

DAYO. I did! I… Okay, ermm… sooo… I'm just here speaking… so you can / you can –

KIERON. JESUS…

DAYO. Find me and yeah, just, still speaking… yoooo… yo – yo – yo… (*Raps.*) Kieron's on the mic and he's feeling bare hype, gonna hit you with some bars that'll make your ass tight –

KIERON. KILL ME NOW.

DAYO. They were your bars, not mine!

KIERON. I don't wanna be stuck here in darkness Dayo!!

DAYO. But I'm here! (*Beat.*) Sounds like you're getting closer!…

KIERON. Yeah?

DAYO. Yeah, you got this! Just come to my voice… I'm here… I'm here. (*Long beat.*) Why won't you open it?… The box?…

KIERON. Ohhhhh / myyy –

DAYO. I don't get what you're afraid of –

KIERON. Right now? Slamming my face into a wall.

DAYO. It's important. You can't just leave it, pretend like it's not here, like it never existed… like you did with –

Lights shoot back on to reveal a tableau of: KIERON *leant over the table, a stern gesture towards* DAYO. ADEYEYE, *a few paces away from* KIERON, *his hands reaching towards him for connection, and a subdued* DAYO, *a gesture reflecting his internal questions. We hold this for a moment, then* KIERON *shoots off.*

Wait!…

KIERON *stops.* DAYO *goes over to the box, hands it to* KIERON. *He glares at it for a beat.* ADEYEYE*'s body rises with hope…*

KIERON. You were good. With me gone and that. You were good.

ADEYEYE *deflates, then takes a deep breath in and launches into a boxing motif during the text below. At times,* KIERON *synchronises with him, infusing the motif with added intensity. Amidst this,* ADEYEYE*'s body succumbs to moments of pain, yet* KIERON *persists with the motif.*

DAYO. Is that a question?

KIERON. Life is gonna throw punches at you no matter how old you are, or what you think you deserve. I thought I deserved to be on the track and field, waving that flag in the Olympics – **BANG!** Uppercut to the chin – change of plan. It's what you do with them… what you do with the punches and the ones you throw back. You're standing here, which means you threw back. You were good. And… he was, too.

A moment. A despondent ADEYEYE *retreats.* KIERON *jolts towards him.*

You carry on?

DAYO. Huh?

KIERON (*shifts back to* DAYO). Singing. Did he carry on?

DAYO. Wouldn't leave hospital visits without serenading at least two doctors.

KIERON. My heart goes out to God. He must be getting an earful!

DAYO. From Burna Boy, to Usher…

KIERON. Ohhh myyy dayssss Usher?!?!

DAYO. You remember?!

KIERON. Remember?! Those bedroom shows?! Day in, day out, causing a racket!!!

ADEYEYE *stands. Licks his lips. Ohhh he's feeling himself. 'Superstar (Interlude)' by Usher begins. He mimes the words over…*

Granted, *Confessions* is arguably one the greatest R&B albums ever made…

DAYO. Bar none…

KIERON. But hearing anything fifty times a day will make you sick of it!

Ocean waves flood us into 'Superstar' by Usher. Lights change…

SHOWTIME.

ADEYEYE *takes centre-stage. Arena-show vibes. On each 'you' at the start of the track,* ADEYEYE *points at a female member in the audience. Also, just before the lyric 'bodyguards',* KIERON *and* DAYO *become bodyguards and* ADEYEYE *gestures at them. After the first chorus, ocean waves merge with the music and sweep us out of this moment.*

DAYO. The way he just lit up.

KIERON. And you lit up right there with him! Geeing him on with that smile of yours!

DAYO. I liked seeing him like that! Him feeling good, made *me* feel good. How about you?… What makes *you* feel good? (*Long beat.*) If you had your own *Confessions* album, what would the track list be?

KIERON. I ain't got nothing to confess!

DAYO. Excuse me, but if Usher, arguably the most perfect Black man to ever grace this earth, has confessions… we all do.

KIERON. Start it off then, innit!

DAYO. You can't just flip it onto / me!

KIERON. Well there you go then! (*Beat.*) Nah, I'm clean, man… I'm clean.

Beat. DAYO *shifts to his plate of food. Eats.*

DAYO. 'D'. Title of the first track on mine.

KIERON. 'D'?… That's it?!…

DAYO *nods.*

And that stands for…

DAYO. Just 'D'.

KIERON. Just –

ADEYEYE (*from his position*). D!!!… D!!!…

Lights shift. DAYO *drops down. Sits with a dictionary. Reads it one moment, then glances away the next, tries to memorise what he reads.* ADEYEYE *sits with headphones on and a CD player in hand. They are in separate rooms, but the same house.* ADEYEYE *frustratingly takes the headphones out. Plugs and replugs… No luck.*

D!… D!…

DAYO. Yeahhhh!!

ADEYEYE. Cooooooooome!!

DAYO. What's / wrong?!

ADEYEYE. I knew I should have got the Sony one!!! Come, man, I need you to fix this damn –

DAYO. Okay, just – just I wanna finish this last –

ADEYEYE. Pleassseeeeee!!!

DAYO. JUST ONE MINUTE!!!

Beat. ADEYEYE*'s body shifts, or,* *__he__* *shifts it.*

ADEYEYE. Ahhh… my neck… my neck!… D!!… D!!… My neck, man!…

DAYO *looks up, stands. He looks torn, but sits back down and carries on reading.*

DAYO, I'm serious! My neck! I need you! I need you!!… D!… D!… D!… D!… D!… D!…

During the 'Ds', lights fade onto DAYO *as he continues reading while ignoring* ADEYEYE*'s cries for help. Simultaneously, his body convulses as if each 'D' were a dagger penetrating his chest, revealing his increasing agitation and inner struggle.*

Ocean waves sweep us out of this memory – KIERON *bursts in, performing some kind of throw.* DAYO *exits into the closet. Lights shift – back into the room.*

KIERON *looks out and continues… Holds an imaginary object in his right hand, throws and repeats. A javelin throw.* DAYO *rummages in the closet offstage.*

DAYO (*offstage*). It weren't that deep!

KIERON. Course it weren't, to you! Walkin round in that fluffy white wool…

DAYO (*offstage*). What?!

KIERON. It's cool! I liked being the black sheep! I always tell my students, it's good to be different, against the grain. Just… all the stuff around it, was… even the way Mum was with you, him… especially him…

DAYO *enters, gently rolls a tennis ball between his hands.*

DAYO. She had to be like that with him. We all did. If anyone felt like the odd one out, don't you think it was / him?!

KIERON. He slyly loved it! Knew how to get everyone focused on him! Even admitted it to me one time!

DAYO. The way you talk about it… about *him*, / it's like –

KIERON. Remember school! Him and that mouth of his!!

ADEYEYE *springs up and directs the following to* KIERON.

ADEYEYE. But look at your crusty lips though! They double up as a cheese-grater!

DAYO. He was the only person I ever saw that made you stutter!

KIERON (*to* ADEYEYE). If my lips double up as a cheese-grater, your forehead doubles up as a runway! (*To* DAYO.) Man never stuttered.

ADEYEYE. *My* forehead?! Blud your forehead is so big even Dora can't explore it.

DAYO. Most of your cusses were on point, but for some reason, he always got you / stuttering –

KIERON (*to* ADEYEYE). Dora yeah?! Dora?! Talking to me about – okay – but but but but – what about your hairline though?!… I bet it comes home fifteen minutes after you do!!!

ADEYEYE *sits back down.* KIERON *turns back fully to a grinning* DAYO. *Beat.*

Shut up, man, that's not stuttering… I was thinking innit. (*Beat.*) The way his mouth got me mad. And you, always there by his side.

DAYO. But… I'd come to you. I'd always come and try and calm you down when things got –

KIERON. You're remembering wrong. You were stuck by his side the whole time, smiling that smile of yours and it got me bare…

KIERON *tenses with frustration. Suddenly,* DAYO *throws the ball to* KIERON, *which catches him off-guard and jolts him from his state.* KIERON *catches it, looks at it for a moment, then, up to* DAYO. *Beat. He throws it back, and they begin to throw the ball to each other in silence. This will happen at least three times before* DAYO *speaks, and then continues over below.*

DAYO. I know it was you. Week by week seeing my pees dip lower and lower…

KIERON. What you talking about?

DAYO. Took time and energy you know! I know for a fact it was you. (*Beat.*) My Bart Simpson piggy bank. I know it was you.

KIERON. Ohhh myyy – you still think it / was – !!?!

DAYO. YEP!

KIERON. Grown-ass man crying over a couple pennies ya na!

DAYO. Thirty-five pounds, fifty-two pence, to be exact.

KIERON. Wow.

DAYO. That was a lot back then! (*Beat.*) Bart Simpson. Track one of your *Confessions* album.

Beat.

KIERON. Welcome to the club by the way. (*Gestures to his head.*) I still think back to the dreams I had of growing locks. Man went from a thick head of hair, to bald as a blud –

DAYO. I still don't get how he went through everything he did, but still had a full head of hair! Must be all that laughing. When did yours start?

KIERON. A month after I left.

Beat. KIERON *approaches* DAYO, *grabs his head and examines it harshly.*

Flakes, upon flakes, upon – when's the last time you washed it?!

DAYO. Two weeks ago – ish.

KIERON. Just 'cause you gone bald don't mean you stop…?! Jesus. You at least do it the way I show you?… You don't forget these life lessons!

DAYO. I never did.

ADEYEYE *dips his hands in the casket. Starts over to* KIERON.

KIERON. I still remember that day… catching him washing his hair with… I can't even say it… I might vomit.

DAYO. Radox!!

KIERON. Radox ya na! On a Black man's hair!!

DAYO. Yanked it from him and –

ADEYEYE *passes water from his hands to* KIERON*'s.* KIERON *then gently runs his fingers through* ADEYEYE*'s hair. This simple gesture evolves into an intimate duet, focusing on their hands and heads.*

It was the first and last time I saw you like that with him. You were locked in… your hands… they were so… in that moment, he was the most important thing in the world. (*Beat.*) But as the days…

The duet becomes more abrasive, over –

KIERON. Dabs –

DAYO. Weeks…

KIERON. Wait –

DAYO. Months…

KIERON. MOVE!

DAYO. Brothers in arms, into brothers *at* them…

ADEYEYE *and* KIERON *break into a stand-off. The sequence ends with a stylised push by* KIERON, *which contorts* ADEYEYE*'s body. An important moment.*

…then that moment. Three days in the hospital and no more ring time. It was a miracle it wasn't worse, especially in his condition. I always wanted to know, if you could –

Lights change. Back in the room. KIERON *shoots to the mop and starts to frantically clean.*

KIERON. *Why* you bringing this up?! Digging into ground that is dry and set! Let it be!

DAYO. But I wanna know if you could go –

KIERON. LET. IT. BE.

DAYO. *The problem with comprehension, is it often comes too late…*

KIERON. What?!

DAYO. Something I read.

KIERON. Course you did.

DAYO. If you could go back would you have / changed –

KIERON. There's no going back! There's only what's now and what's next.

DAYO. So what's next? With you, *us*?

KIERON. What's next, is what's now! This! Us! Here! Talking!… This is good!

DAYO. This is surface.

KIERON. This is enough.

DAYO. Feels like there's things we need to… Like there's unfinished business, and I wanna leave here knowing that I've, / that we've –

KIERON. He's gone, man, he's…!! Whether you like it or not it's finished.

Beat. DAYO *gets a text. Takes phone out, reads.*

I see your phone managed to charge itself!

DAYO. Mum's looking for me.

DAYO *starts off.* KIERON *shoots over to him.*

The following action/movement will happen simultaneously as KIERON *speaks…*

ADEYEYE *dips his hand in the casket, approaches* KIERON, *and reaches out for his hand.* KIERON *yanks it away without acknowledging him.*

This builds into movement: ADEYEYE *strives to lead* KIERON *to the casket, yet* KIERON *remains resistant. During this, he persists in trying to maintain eye contact with* DAYO.

Hey… It's like you said in your speech… he always saw the good in everything, right? Said you're gonna try reach for it, while you're still here on earth, for him. We gotta grab and hold on to whatever good we can and not look back. It's not easy, but it's life, Dayo… it's not supposed to be and you dragging up the past, you might not realise it right now, but you doing that is taking the easy way out. No regrets, no regression. We move.

DAYO. And you're *good*?

Beat. The movement crescendoes. KIERON *dashes away, and goes straight into –*

KIERON. Course I'm good!!… Well, obviously, not with… But yeah… I'm good.

A dismayed ADEYEYE *steps back.* DAYO *starts off, then stops at the door. Takes his phone out.*

DAYO. She wants to speak with you. Mum.

KIERON. What?

DAYO. Told her I'm with you and she text back saying she wants / to –

KIERON. Why?!… Why does she – nah nah nah – I'm about to – to / tell her to –

DAYO. I'll bring her in / yeah?

KIERON. NO!!… We're about to – to leave, so there's no point – tell her… just tell her another time.

DAYO (*beat*). Yeah. You're good.

KIERON *looks confused.* DAYO *starts off.*

She didn't text. I lied.

KIERON. You think that's funny?… You think lies are funny?

DAYO (*stops*). I just wanted to show you –

KIERON. Show me what?! Show me *you*?! Oh, I see you Dayo, I see you loud and clear.

DAYO. Do you?

KIERON. You! Of all people?! You! / Shouldn't be surprised.

DAYO. Don't you think you're overreacting a bit?

KIERON. You're just like them! Pathetic / absolutely pathetic!!

DAYO. Yo relax! I only did it to show you that you're / not as good as you –

KIERON. YOU DON'T LIE TO PEOPLE DAYO YOU DON'T LIE <u>THEY RUIN LIVES</u>!!!

KIERON *darts off – exits.* DAYO *rushes over to the food, takes a bite and chews aggressively. He eyes the casket… lights gently rise on it and* ADEYEYE.

DAYO. I'm all ears, tell me!! How do I make him *see*? And how do I stop myself drowning in it?!… I meant it, I wanna reach for that good, right here, right now on this earth, but *this earth*, man!! (*Beat.*) What's it like up there, bro?…

ADEYEYE *smiles, inhales deeply, then exhales. On the exhale, the tension releases from* DAYO *and they fluidly exchange positions through movement.* DAYO *now stands closer to the casket.*

Bet you got Burna Boy on repeat, as you, Sugar Ray, Frazier and Ali go toe-to-toe! Bussin out into song whenever you feel! That's your heaven in a nutshell, innit!!…

ADEYEYE *meaningfully inhales and exhales.*

What would mine be like?… No pearly white gates, no six-foot bearded white man… got enough of them in Hackney already thanks. In my heaven… Timmy would be on a podium playing his violin, letting the dulcet tones pulsate through his body and into Bola's, who grins his teeth as he takes out his award-winning spiced rum cake from the oven, slices it and hands it to Cory, who chucks it to the side 'cause he's too busy tryna find the perfect light for his portrait, lifts his eye from his camera to find me… walking past as I conjure up any book just by thinking of the title! There'd be a sea of books!… There'd be a sea of <u>Black boys</u>, standing with our chins up, shoulders loose, surrounded by rays of light, letting the feeling catch us… Letting it catch me… chin up shoulders loose, and let it catch me… **chin up shoulders loose**, and let it catch me – **chin up**, **shoulders loose** and let it **catch me** – let it **catch me** – let it…

'Spirit 2.0' by Sampha begins, to be timed immediately after the final 'let it'. Movement begins to swell from his body…

ADEYEYE *seamlessly enters into parts of* DAYO*'s movement as it builds. The heart of this is all about letting the rhythm, the feeling catch these Black men. A reclamation of identity through every step and revelling fully in it. Make no mistake: this, in itself, is a political act. The track fades down after the first verse and chorus.*

Your *good*, your laugh, told me it's possible to let the fear go, and let the light catch me, on earth… but first, I gotta face the things I felt towards you. Gotta face the lies… the times I told you I couldn't pick you up from hospital, 'cause I was working when really, I was… Saying 'I'm fine' when you asked, but looking at you with a two-tonne feeling in my… I gotta face it all! Gotta face myself, the world, *him* and it's all so messy! I know that laugh lives inside my body, but it feels so **messy**!

DAYO *tenses.* ADEYEYE *runs to the casket, dips his hands in and approaches* DAYO *with slow and deliberate steps. Now face to face with him, he reaches out – an offering.* DAYO *reaches back, and they connect hands, transferring the water.* ADEYEYE *then begins a set of meaningful movements with his chest and arms… A cleansing ritual.* DAYO *picks up shards of it in his body, as he starts towards the casket, when –*

Lights change. Back to the room. KIERON *peeks through the door.*

KIERON. I'm off. Might wanna get your Tupperware out, the aunties are out in full force. (*Beat.*) Look, Dayo, this is life… real life. We all just / gotta –

DAYO *starts laughing. His laugh builds and builds.* KIERON *looks at him, baffled.*

DAYO. LIFE!!… REAL LIFE!!!…

You know that laugh where you feel like you're doing twenty ab-crunches at once? That's DAYO *right now. He jumps up, prepares for something, but can't stop laughing. The laugh he's wanted to do for so long. He tries to compose himself.*

Okay – nah – wait – wait – wait – okay – nah – wait – wait – okay – okay – okay –

KIERON. Are *you* okay?!?!

DAYO *calms. Takes a deep breath in, and…*

DAYO. 'Behold, Semmi. Life!… Real life!! A thing that we have been denied for far too long!… Good morning, my neighbours!!!…'

DAYO *looks at* KIERON… *Nothing. Goes again…*

'Good morning, my neighbours!!…'

Still nothing.

'Good – '

KIERON. 'HEY, FUCK YOU!!!'

DAYO. 'YES! YES! FUCK – YOU – TOO!!'

They laugh. Beat.

KIERON. Heard the second one was dead.

DAYO. Didn't watch it either! No way I was letting anything taint that memory. Us sitting together, with a sea of food.

KIERON (*starts off*). Yeah… well…

DAYO. What's your favorite moment? In *Coming to America*… tell me this then you can go.

KIERON. There's only one. (*Impersonating line from film.*) 'Your royal penis is clean, your highness.' The way she rises up from the water… like it was nothing…

DAYO. I mean, yeah, that was good, but that's not *the* moment…

ADEYEYE *stands with a grin.*

KIERON. Nothing tops that!

Ocean waves take us into: an empty spotlight. After a long beat, ADEYEYE *calmly steps into it. He takes a deep breath in and enacts the following moment from the film – pitch and movement perfect.*

ADEYEYE (*singing*). 'Sheeeee's yourrrr Queeeen-to-Beeeee!! A queen-to-be forever a queen who'll do whatever, his highness desires… sheeee's yourrrrr…'

Lights widen to reveal DAYO *and* KIERON *silently belly-laughing in slow motion. Ocean waves sweep us out of the moment – back to the room.*

DAYO. We had moments. And we can make new ones. Right here, right now…

KIERON. Your mind, man, it's crazy how your mind's just blocked out all the –

DAYO. *Little Mermaid*!

KIERON. Huh?!

DAYO. 'Under the Sea'… another moment!

KIERON. I'm still tryna rub that whole situation from my / memory.

DAYO. Remember the routine?

KIERON. NO I DO NOT. I DO NOT REMEMBER ANYTHING. MOVE ON.

DAYO. Wood Green Chinese Buffet, after church…
I remember eating so much and smiling, laughing so hard whenever we went! You too.

KIERON. But how did it always end?

DAYO. Not always. It weren't his fault / he was in pain.

KIERON. Hmmmm.

DAYO. Whenever he lifts –

ADEYEYE *drifts centre-stage. Perhaps simulates below, in slow motion.*

Lifted his shoulders up to his ears and tilted his head back, it was serious. He was having a pain crisis / so we had to –

KIERON. The last time we ever went, maybe it was just a bit of a coincidence, but literally one minute before he started to have his pain crisis, he was crying his eyes out 'cause Dad wouldn't give him more Fanta. His shoulders weren't up to his ears then.

DAYO. Nah, you're remembering wrong / he was –

KIERON. You remember words, I remember pictures.
I remember that one clear as day.

DAYO. I'm telling you, he was –

KIERON. It was *my* birthday!! (*Beat.*) Moments, right?… Laughing, having a good time, but they always got cut short, even on my… And those cut-off moments add up.

DAYO. You could handle it!

KIERON. Yeah / well…

DAYO. Everyone knew you could! Always kept your head down, kept yourself to yourself – just got on with things! You were solid!

KIERON. I know! And that's – that's the key to life! Gotta… That's why I stopped going to Mum with any problems I had, 'cause she obviously expected me to – she knew I could just get on with it, and I could! I did!… All I'm saying is, I don't get why no one wanted to see the whole picture, with him. Why everyone automatically believed him and not… how your whole life can turn within the space of a moment, especially when that moment has two versions, just like **that** –

Whatever physical gesture KIERON *does on 'that' makes the lights snap change and* ADEYEYE *freeze. Then, when* DAYO *speaks, lights slowly cross-fade back to their previous state and* ADEYEYE *continues.*

DAYO (*beat*). He tried. Tried to reach out, after you left… to start afresh…

KIERON *does another gesture. Lights shift, but slowly fade back to their previous state… the worlds start to collide.*

Remember that day he travelled all the way / to –

KIERON. Nahhh I don't wanna… let's get out of this, / this ain't real…

Another abrupt gesture from KIERON, *but nothing happens. Frustrated, he tries something else… a clap, a click, a stomp, anything to make this moment stop.*

DAYO. Saw him from your window and left him out there to freeze, in his state.

KIERON. That was his choice! He was aware of his state. We all were / constantly.

DAYO. He didn't choose to have sickle cell! Me and you, we won the lottery!

KIERON. You can win the lottery and still feel poor.

DAYO. His blood transfusion two years ago and you didn't / even –

KIERON. This ain't real! He's not here and this ain't –

DAYO. Yes he is! If you just look, you'll / see!!!

KIERON. I SAID LET'S GET OUT OF THIS!!!

He aggressively does another gesture, which, this time, snaps us out of this moment. Lights simultaneously change onto…

ADEYEYE. *He takes a breath in, and snaps into where he left off with his boxing. This brief and final solo is about him finding acceptance in his body as it is, as* he *is, boxing in pain, yet with a smile. The sequence crescendoes…*

ADEYEYE *leans over, then falls to the ground, weakened.* DAYO *runs over, tries to hold him up, but* ADEYEYE *collapses over and over again.* DAYO *continues, but* ADEYEYE *eventually stands on his own volition. He separates himself from* DAYO *and walks to the casket, a silent summons for* DAYO *to follow.*

And DAYO *does, he picks up where he left off with the cleansing ritual, getting closer to the casket than he ever has, when –*

A riled-up KIERON *bursts into the space, snapping us out of this moment. Lights shift. Back to the room.* DAYO *rushes towards* KIERON, *attempting to quell his rage.*

AIN'T LOOKED AT ME ONCE YA NA! WOMAN AIN'T LOOKED AT ME / ONCE! AND THE ONE TIME SHE DOES…!!

DAYO. Just calm down!! You know what she's / like!

KIERON. If it was just me and her I wouldn't give a shit!! But to do that in front of Martina, in front of / Akin?!

DAYO. Don't let her get you all / riled up!!

KIERON. In front of my family!!! To do that in front of / my…?!?!

KIERON *drops to the floor, aggressively does press-ups, during:*

DAYO. She's your family too!

KIERON. That witch ain't my family! Aunty Funke?! Aunty Fuck'ry more like!

DAYO. Come on, you can't be speaking / like that!

KIERON. Family don't look at family with those eyes!!! (*Beat.*) They wanna see me drown, man… they wanna see me… (*Shoots up.*) I knew I should have left after the church! The only reason I stayed for you ya na!

DAYO. Me?… What about / *him*?

KIERON. Yeah, obviously – that goes without… in front of my family though?! Looking at me with those same eyes from all those… kissing your dutty teeth at me, in front of my… Nahhhh… nah – nah – nah – nah – nah – I ain't having that! NO WAY!!!

He shoots towards the door. DAYO *blocks him.*

DAYO. No no no! Please, just leave it! / This ain't the right – just calm down!

KIERON. MOVE!! I'm serious!! No way she's getting away with that! I gotta make her see man – gotta make them all – DAYO, I will straight up yank you from the door if you don't –

DAYO *suddenly bursts into a repeated movement that looks… well, a bit weird to say the least.* KIERON *glances over, baffled.* DAYO *repeats it.* KIERON *kisses his teeth, bolts towards the door again. The below dialogue should play out like an extension of their argument.*

DAYO (*does the movement with the words*). SHOULDER BOP, SHOULDER BOP, SPRINKLE / SPRINKLE UP!!!

KIERON. MOVE!!!

DAYO. SHOULDER BOP, SHOULDER BOP, SPRINKLE / SPRINKLE UP!!!…

KIERON. I AIN'T GONNA ASK YOU / AGAIN!!

DAYO. SHOULDER BOP, SHOULDER BOP –

KIERON. DAYO!!! (*Beat.*) SWOOP SWOOP DOWN… now move!

DAYO. Huh?!

KIERON. SHOULDER BOP, SHOULDER BOP, SWOOP SWOOP <u>DOWN</u>!! There weren't no sprinkle, bruv… you're making up a sprinkle.

DAYO. Whaaaaaaaat?

KIERON. Are you forgetting I choreographed half the ting?! Telling me about a sprinkle…

Beat.

DAYO. You're remembering wrong.

KIERON. I done told you, I remember pictures!!

DAYO. Wellllll I guess there's only one way to find out…

KIERON. DAYO.

DAYO. We gotta know the / truth innit!!

KIERON. Look, I know – listen – I know what you're tryna – no – Dayo, aye!… DAYO!… Nah, I don't… I don't like that look in your eyes, man… Don't you dare… Dayo, don't you – !!

During above, DAYO *approaches* KIERON *with an increasingly bigger grin. He looks up, the lights shift and an underbelly of sound builds…*

Oh God.

And we are fully swept into the instrumental of 'Under the Sea' from The Little Mermaid. ADEYEYE *floats centre-stage,* DAYO *and* KIERON *join him on the left and right… And yes, folks, we are about to witness three grown-ass Black men doing a shitty-yet-joyful dance routine to 'Under the Sea' with a beautiful childlike energy as they were. The sequence ends after the first chorus.*

Lights change. Back to the room.

Alright, fine, it was a sprinkle… whatever innit.

They laugh. DAYO *edges closer to* KIERON. *His body looks like he wants to embrace him.* KIERON *shifts away.*

All this 'going back' business. I know what you're… It stops now. Best believe she's gonna feel me before I leave.

Beat.

Don't look at me like that.

DAYO. Like…?

KIERON. The way everyone behind that door is… like I'm a… Pollock.

DAYO. You do know a pollock's a fish, right?… I think you mean pillock?

KIERON *looks out, his eyes locked on something. He edges closer, over…*

KIERON. I walk past it two, three times a day to get to the staffroom and every time I do… can't not look at it. Kinda haunts me. I keep telling myself, it's just a painting, but… it keeps telling me that it's more.

DAYO. What is it?

KIERON. Splatters of paint. A student did a copy of a piece from that Jackson –

DAYO. Pollock!… Jackson Pollock!…

KIERON. Blues, yellows, reds… wild – messy… searching. It's like the colours are searching, fighting for a home, but… can't find one…

His body softens, DAYO *supports him;* KIERON *then snaps back into rigidity. Nudges* DAYO *off.*

How the hell can splatters of paint on a rhatid piece of paper be worth twenty million pounds?! (*Beat.*) I tell Akin, you'll always have to fight for a space in the world, but you'll never have to fight for a space in your home.

DAYO. I nearly became a dad.

KIERON. What?

DAYO. Shit. Ain't ever told anyone that.

Beat.

KIERON. What happened?

DAYO *goes over to his plate of food, picks at it, but doesn't eat.*

DAYO. She… it was an accident in the first place, but she ended up… like… You know.

KIERON *edges closer to* DAYO*, then stops. Edges back.*

KIERON. This life, man, I swear / this –

DAYO. Do you remember that day? September fifteenth, two years ago?… I called you like six times in a row. You text saying you were busy and will call me back, but… That was the day I found out.

KIERON (*shifts*). Well done though, for you know – getting through it and… for getting hit and – (*Simulates a punch.*) it's the only… so, yeah / well done.

DAYO. What do you feel? Right now. Being here with me?

KIERON.…I'm here innit.

DAYO. That's not a feeling. There's gotta be something, put words to it.

KIERON. For what?!…

DAYO. For / me –

KIERON. They don't even touch the surface anyway!… Can't get within an inch of what I'm…

DAYO. Go on…

KIERON (*shifts*). Feelings, words, book quotes – Jesus, let it go, man!

DAYO. Why are you such a Tetris block?!

KIERON. Huh?!

DAYO. Rigid, four turning-points and no –

KIERON. Hold up, you think this world needs me soft?! Warm and cosy?! Jeeeeesus, I weren't sure, but, yeah… I think you are losing it…

KIERON *limbers his body up.*

DAYO. Losing / it?

KIERON. Lord knows, I can't teach you nothing if you lose it! The world outside?! It will eat you up, spit you out and –

DAYO. I don't care about the world outside! / I just want to see –

KIERON. The world outside is the only thing that matters, especially when the world outside constantly tells you that you don't. That's the foundation that we start with, gotta build on. Imma Tetris block for a reason!… I just pray you don't lose it!

DAYO. Lose what??

BANG!!! The sound of a race gun reverberates around the space. Lights shift. KIERON *runs in slow motion.*

KIERON. I'm on the starting block – PUMPED – ain't ever felt so ready for a race in my life! Strong start – feeling good… last hurdle, front leg up, clears, I'm in the air now and suddenly my body's heavy, 'cause my back foot… my back foot catches the… and before I know it, my neck's weakened, chin's dipped and I'm kissing dirt and that's when I see him pass me… *Him*, of all people. The same him from the locker room waxing lyrical about how too many people who look like us are taking over the sport. That it's easier for us, 'cause we got an extra edge and it ain't fair. I mean, he was right! About that edge, us man are built different and what! But he tried to minus the work… tried to go on like we just wake up and don't fight for it! And in that moment, I knew… I not only had to beat him, but it had to be by a stretch, has to be unquestionable, <u>always</u>. But I buckled, man, over the last… 'cause I didn't have enough of it. And yeah, maybe if I had known it was gonna be my last race before I had to… maybe I would have made sure I had more of it, but it taught me a lesson. You gotta start with it, and never lose it! No matter what, Dayo, don't lose it…

DAYO. Lose what, / man?!?!

KIERON. <u>YOUR ANGER!</u> It's what activates, sharpens us!

DAYO. Then what?

KIERON. Then we make the best music on the fucking planet!! Then we jump higher, throw further, run faster! It's our biggest tool. Exists in us for a reason.

DAYO. At what cost?

KIERON. You can take a horse to water, but you can't make it *think*… Yeah, I got quotes too!

DAYO. I never said I had all the answers!

KIERON. The only answer you need, the only answer that is required is **anger**. It's the one stereotype I'll happily swim deep in! It's in your blood whether you like it or not and blood is thicker than water – it's what keeps you alive! Keeps you winning! Gets you over that final hurdle! And when the time comes, when the world throws you those punches and you're on all fours, back on starting block, that anger's gonna strengthen your neck, lift your chin and stand you back up. It's gonna give you the energy you need to replan your life when people – family, the world turns against you… When you lose your last race, without knowing it was gonna be your last, when you're falling in slow motion and feel like a failure – it's gonna hold you, Dayo!… Gonna hold you when you can't stop replaying the moments – the lies – the eyes – gonna hold you when no one else will, gonna hold you when you don't feel like you can hold your… hold on to it, Dayo please hold on, 'cause what else do I have, if I don't have my… gotta hold on to it, Dayo… please… <u>please</u>…

'Sampha's Plea' by Stormzy begins. KIERON *paces, like a lion separated from his pride.* ADEYEYE *sees his turmoil, dips his hands into the casket, approaches him and extends his hand. The gesture escalates into a grappling duet, bodies twisting and turning – a physical manifestation of* KIERON*'s rage towards* ADEYEYE, *and himself, as well as* ADEYEYE*'s yearning for resolution. The sequence builds until* KIERON *finally seems to soften, if only slightly.*

ADEYEYE *reaches out again, and this time* KIERON *tentatively reciprocates, but still struggles to meet his brother's gaze. Their hands inch closer, achingly close to connection.* KIERON *finally musters the courage to lock eyes with him… their fingertips within touching distance, they are about to connect. But at the last moment,* KIERON *pulls away…*

BLACKOUT.

<u>If</u> there is an interval…

it could be here.

ACT TWO

In blackout, muffled sounds of the sea swell. Each wave grows in clarity, as this boundless sea runs –

Closer… Closer…

The waves sweep the theatre, wash the walls, swish under our feet, runs towards us –

Closer… Closer…

The waves are about to wash right over us…

And –

LIGHTS UP.

DAYO *and* KIERON *stand opposite each other, hands clasped, knees bent, eyes locked… SLAPS.*

ADEYEYE *is sat by the casket and will remain visible in the space for the rest of the piece.*

KIERON *and* DAYO *stay still and silent for a very long beat. It's TENSE. After a beat,* KIERON *shifts his hands,* DAYO *immediately moves his away.*

KIERON. One…

DAYO. WHAT?!?!

KIERON. ONE.

DAYO *huffs, begrudgingly places his hands back. Beat.* KIERON *shifts his hands again –* DAYO *retracts.*

TWO.

DAYO. You can't…?! You're doing exactly / what you used to –

KIERON. My hands are still together –

DAYO. But / you –

KIERON. My hands are still together!

DAYO. How can the game move forward if you / keep doing –

KIERON. Why is your voice high-pitched?… You scared?

DAYO. NO!

KIERON. One more time and I get a free slap!

DAYO. I know the rules! Just – just – just –

KIERON. Who's stuttering now?

They reset. A very long beat.

Drumsticks are on point yeah? I think I might be a bit peckish after this.

DAYO *huffs. Beat.* KIERON *shifts,* DAYO *retracts his hands… SHIT.*

DAYO. NO THAT'S NOT – ?!?! / YOU ALWAYS DO THE SAME – YOU CAN'T – YOU NEVER END UP EVEN PLAYING THE GAME IF YOU –

KIERON. Ohhhhhhhhhhhh / hhhhhhhhhhhhhh shiiiiiiit…

DAYO (*backs off*). Look, man – just – please – not hard, okay? Allow me.

KIERON (*in Yoda voice*). Do I detect some fear…

DAYO. Here we go…

KIERON (*still in Yoda mode*). Fear is the path to the Dark Side, young one. (*Back in his voice.*) Ermmm, you seem to be floating away from our central position…

DAYO *reluctantly returns, visibly shaking.*

Your face is mad sweaty ya na! You know what? Imma be a good sport and let you wipe that dutty sweat from your face, before I slap the black off your hand.

DAYO (*places hands back*). JUST DO IT!!!

KIERON. Alright Nike.

Beat. KIERON *takes a deep breath, raises his hand slowly and intensely above his head… looks like he's truly about to slap the black off* DAYO*'s hand… but, suddenly walks away.*

Remember this.

DAYO (*sigh of relief*). Oh my God – Oh my – thank you Jesus / thank you!!!

KIERON. It's me you should be thanking!

DAYO. If this was back in the day, boy… you're definitely getting old.

KIERON. The night is still young.

DAYO. He'd be proud.

Beat. KIERON *shifts.* DAYO *looks up, lets out a sombre sigh.* KIERON *feels the weight of this moment, too. Then, he suddenly shoots off with a determined streak…*

KIERON. One sec…

…Exits and leaves a baffled DAYO. *The music that plays from the hi-fi system fades down, and 'Ye' by Burna Boy fades up, LOUD.* DAYO *smiles. Lights rise on* ADEYEYE *who also beams.* KIERON *re-enters.*

You know what time it is!

DAYO. What?!

KIERON. Let's go!!

DAYO. Allow it, man, I don't –

KIERON. Let's see that infamous foot shuffle then! He's watching!! (*Claps.*) OYA!!!

After a beat, DAYO *starts to bop his shoulders. This bop grows into his chest, arms, head, until he eventually starts to… BRUK OUUUUUT!*

The track fades into our main speakers. A hyped ADEYEYE *dances and passionately mouths every single lyric.*

KIERON *takes out a stack of one-dollar bills and playfully dabs them on* DAYO*'s forehead… an act known as 'spraying' in Nigerian culture.* DAYO *gestures* KIERON *to join him, but* KIERON *strongly resists. He does not dance; he will not dance – NOPE. But* DAYO *keeps goading him,* *and eventually,* KIERON *squeezes out a small, brief shuffle, then shakes it off and walks away… that's all you're getting.*

KIERON *nudges* DAYO *towards the door, wanting him to share his moves on the main dance floor in the hall.* DAYO *smiles and heads to it, dancing as he goes, then turns and gestures for* KIERON *to join him.* KIERON *shrugs.* DAYO *gestures again, then exits.* KIERON *looks out, takes a deep breath of courage, and exits.*

As soon as he does, the music reverberates slightly as we're left with ADEYEYE, *who goes toward the door, watching what unfolds offstage with joyful shuffles. After a beat, he hurries back to the casket. The music fades.*

KIERON *enters and starts to pick up the dollar bills, then stops, glancing at the wooden box for a beat. Then* DAYO *enters, and* KIERON *snaps his gaze away, continuing to pick up the bills in silence for a beat.*

That smile, man. The space around you just… opens up. (*Beat.*) I'd swap these shoulders for that smile, in a heartbeat.

DAYO (*beat*). I missed you.

KIERON *goes to the mop and cleans, as if he didn't hear those three words. This hits* DAYO *hard. He shakes his head and starts off.*

I think I'm gonna…

KIERON *jolts, stops mopping.*

KIERON. Wait!

DAYO *stops.* KIERON *goes to say something, but stops himself, instead, takes his phone out.*

You on Monzo?

DAYO. Ermm… yeah?

KIERON *types on his phone, then, ping!* DAYO *receives a message… takes his phone out.*

Why you sending me thirty-five pounds, fifty… two… I knew it was you!!

KIERON *laughs.*

I flippin…!! Ohh myyyy… By the way, in line with inflation, you should be adding another zero to that!

KIERON. If you knew it was me, why didn't you press me harder?

DAYO. I asked you a couple times and you said no… I didn't want to… if you needed money, you should have just asked me / I would have –

KIERON. That's not what an older brother does.

Beat.

DAYO. I thought it might speed up the process. Why I didn't press you on it…

KIERON. The process of what?

DAYO. Your change. Your distance. If I caught you in the lie, then you'd double down. Once you left, I put two and two together that you must have taken it for that, but, before you did… so much changed. No more gym sessions, no more beatboxing to your freestyles, no more morning punch in the chest…

KIERON. You missed me punching you?

DAYO. No / but…

KIERON. If you want me to punch you, I can / punch you.

DAYO. I just mean, you kinda had this numbness / about you.

KIERON. People change because circumstances – because they have to, because – anyway, don't go on like it was just – even before everything happened with me and him – you were jammin round him more / and –

DAYO. 'Cause he got worse he needed me / to –

KIERON. You two and your secret handshakes and talking in that stupid-ass back slang that I still, to this day, do not understand! (*Beat.*) Maybe *you* were the one who changed!

DAYO. Because *he* did. I changed because he…

DAYO *stops, slips into a realisation. Shifts to his plate of food, goes to grab some, but stops himself. Beat.*

KIERON. I was still there.

Beat.

DAYO. You're more van Gogh, than Pollock. There's some paintings you can take in from afar, get a sense of them, then move on, but ones like van Gogh? The closer you get… start to see the shapes behind the shape, the colours beneath the colour. The closer you get, the more you see. (*Beat.*) Do you see anything different? Right here, right now? Him… me?

Their eyes connect, then DAYO*'s flick to the box, drawing* KIERON*'s attention to it too. Their eyes remain locked on the box for a weighted moment.* DAYO*'s stare returns to* KIERON, *who averts his gaze.* DAYO *shoots up, snatches the box and drives it into* KIERON*'s space. He remains stone-faced, refusing to acknowledge it.*

You know what?!… *I'll* do it! There's no way I'm just leaving it here to rot!

KIERON. DON'T YOU DARE!!!

DAYO. IT'S DISRESPECTFUL, MAN, IT'S…!!!

KIERON. So you do have it inside you!

DAYO. But you don't / even wanna –

KIERON. IT AIN'T YOURS TO OPEN IT AIN'T YOURS!!!

KIERON *grabs the box from* DAYO. *Then, after a beat, he looks down and realises the box is actually in his hands. He jolts, quickly placing it on the table, then rushes to the mop and cleans frantically. Beat.*

DAYO. I think it's clean now. Kieron, it's –

KIERON. I'll tell you whether it's clean or not! (*Beat.*) No matter what I do, they'll always be stuck on *him*.

DAYO. Adeyeye?

KIERON. *Me*. They'll always be stuck on this version of me that they think I am… even if I scream in their faces that that's not me, they'll just nod and smile, with those eyes, looking at me like I'm the hardest man on the planet, but if they looked harder, they'd see… Just don't get why they won't look harder, man. (*Beat.*) Life is funny. Got no control of the family you're born into, but that family ends up becoming the story of your life, you spend your lifetime trying to…

KIERON *continues mopping frantically. Beat.*

DAYO. Life ain't funny, but *we* are. I swear, us humans… we do some funny shit. We tell ourselves these… stories to make us sleep at night, make us do terrible things to the planet, to people, but we also tell these stories that make us do terrible things to ourselves. And we don't even realise the damage it's doing, and before you know it, you're –

KIERON. Stories make us who we are.

DAYO. Did you know, this is mad, but I swear, it's legit… did you know that the UK has a minister for loneliness? Yep! Our beloved UK government was the first in the world to publish this 'Loneliness Reduction Strategy' ting. I can just imagine bruddas in the hood laughing their asses off at that, like I did. Then… not.

KIERON. Yeah, well, loneliness is a next ting. But you can be alone… that's different. You're in control of being alone.

KIERON *shifts, glances at his watch.*

DAYO. The only thing you can control is where you put your attention.

KIERON. I kinda like that one. Which one of your books is that from?

DAYO. My therapist.

KIERON. Huh?

DAYO. She said that to me in our last session. Kinda stuck with me. It's tricky though, 'cause where you put your attention, might –

KIERON. Therapy???

DAYO. Yeah. It's only been like a month, but –

KIERON. Rahhh.

DAYO. What?

KIERON (*long beat*). What's wrong?

DAYO. What's…?

KIERON. I mean, yeah there's some cases, some… certain people, when they're proper, you know, and I get it. But you?

DAYO. Me?

KIERON. *Us?*

DAYO. I don't get what the / big deal –

KIERON. You know, back in the day, our ancestors! If they had any issues with people, or – or – themselves… whatever! They'd go straight to the elders, sit in a circle, hash it out!

DAYO. Sounds so simple.

KIERON. Sitting there spilling your life out to some stranger, hoping for what? Clarity? Insight?! You got that all around you! Buck up with you boys! Talk to fam!

DAYO. Pick up the phone and talk to you, yeah?

KIERON. How much they charge you for that anyway?

DAYO. Yeah, it's not… sixty-five an hour…

KIERON. Jeeeeeesus! Shelling out sixty-five a month, ya na!

DAYO. A week.

KIERON. RAHTID!!!

DAYO. Tried going through the NHS, but even just getting a phone consultation / was a –

KIERON. Okay – look – let's – let's, go on…

DAYO. What?

KIERON. What's wrong?… Like… with you… let's go! Let's hash it out!

DAYO. It doesn't work like / that.

KIERON. It works the way you want it to! It's because of this, innit?

DAYO. Him going was the catalyst, but it weren't the cause. It made me stop and realise the weight of it all.

KIERON. What weight?

DAYO. Feels too heavy to ignore now.

KIERON. It's only heavy if you *think* it's heavy!

DAYO. But, my body…

KIERON. It's all in the mind!

DAYO. But, *my body…*

KIERON. Your body what?!

DAYO. **Remembers!!!**

As DAYO*'s words linger, the three brothers align in the space. Movement swells from their bodies as joyful memories from earlier in the piece seep into their gestures and joint physicality. But these joyful flashes bleed into trapped experiences – frantic self-pats, as if being frisked. 'Hands up, don't shoot' postures exploding from them. Their frames shifting between lightness and survival. And as they move, it becomes evident that their bodies, in their silent observance, keep score.*

I wanna look at the stuff it remembers now and start to –

KIERON *breaks out of the movement.*

KIERON. We gotta get out of this rut – this narrative – it's boring now! We ain't broken, we're warriors!!!

DAYO. Even warriors take their armour off before they sleep.

KIERON. Exactly! Take it off at home, not in front of some stranger!

DAYO. What if home is one of the reasons you've got it on in the first place?

KIERON. Making wounds appear out of thin air.

DAYO. Forget wounds! What if it's more like… thousands of little paper cuts you've collected over your lifetime, and your body isn't equipped to heal from them fast enough.

KIERON. Put your mind to it and you can heal from anything.

DAYO. So you can look yourself in the mirror, **in the water** – and say you're fully healed from what you did to him?!

KIERON *stirs, then charges at* DAYO, *gets right in his face. Beat. He shoots out, leaving an enraged* DAYO.

WHY CAN'T HE JUST…?!?!

DAYO *looks at the casket. Lights rise on it.* ADEYEYE *dips his hands in. Looks at* DAYO *with soft eyes.*

If he won't, then… I will…

ADEYEYE *starts to hum 'Amazing Grace'.* DAYO *takes slow and deliberate steps towards him. He stops a few inches away, fearful.*

But… what if I drown?

ADEYEYE. **My brother, what if you rise?**

DAYO*'s body and heart open. He takes his final steps to the casket. Kneels down and dips his hands in it…*

There is something distinctly different about the tone of the below. Something understated, as he truly works things out in the moment, as if speaking these thoughts to a friend, confidant, brother, sat right next to him. Intimate.

Before you passed… I carried on with our Saturdays, even when you couldn't. I had to find a moment, between the hospital visits, work, helping Mum with shopping, between all the bouncing, I had to find a day, regardless if it was a Saturday.

I couldn't do it in Vikki Park 'cause it felt weird, so I'd go London Fields, somewhere I wouldn't be clocked and hit up Uber Eats! Either burgers, or Chinese! I'm talking two, three meals and I'd tuck in!! I'd keep eating and eating and once I was full… (*Beat.*) Once I'm full… I eat a bit more… and a bit more… 'Cause once my body is packed up with food, it feels like I can feel it again. My body would remember being with you on all those Saturdays, all those Chinese buffets. In that moment, my body would taste more than the food, it tastes joy. Love. I'd feel held. Who wouldn't want to cling on to that? Especially when it feels like it's rationed! So I do… one day, turns into two, two into three, three into… eating and eating more than my body wants, just to feel what my body *needs*. Chasing those feelings, but they always slip away and before you know it, you're lost at sea, suffering in silence, suffocating on your own breath! But something inside me knows there's more. Something inside me knows it'll hold me, if I just let it / wash over me…

ADEYEYE. **Wash over you –**

DAYO. Cleanse me… but it feels so hard to / let go –

ADEYEYE. **Let go –**

DAYO. And even harder to / **start again** –

ADEYEYE. **Start again –**

DAYO. But something inside me knows it'll / **cleanse me** –

ADEYEYE. **Cleanse you –**

DAYO. Something inside me knows it'll help me close the gap between who I am, who I say I am, and who I want to be… if I just let it / **wash over me** –

ADEYEYE. **Wash over you** –

DAYO. Cleanse me!… Wash over me… **Cleanse me… wash over me… Cleanse me… Wash over me… cleanse me!**

He drops both hands into the water. Eyes closed. And then, for the first time, enacts the cleansing ritual in its entirety. Opens his eyes…

Now, I see… Joy, love… are supposed to be received, given, shared. I turned that moment of joy we shared together and all the previous ones, into a secret, lonely kind of joy. Clinging on, 'cause I felt like I had nothing else. Clinging on, 'cause when you were here, when you got worse, I hated it! Hated that I couldn't look you in the eye and smile any

more! Laugh any more. I know you didn't choose that life! I know I won the lottery, but the life chosen for you, made me lose options for mine and… a small part of me despised you for that. And that small part of me that despised you, made me despise *all* of me, but I don't wanna float any more, and I don't wanna sit back and watch Kieron drown –
I wanna plant my feet on the ground and let my body fill up with that feeling from the inside, so I surrender!…
I surrender the blame, the shame, the hurt… I surrender it all to the water and I… I… I forgive myself!! (*Beat.*) **I forgive myself.**

DAYO *turns to* ADEYEYE. *His movement expressing the words…*

Do you forgive me???… Do you forgive me?

ADEYEYE *takes a moment, then…*

ADEYEYE. **I forgive you.**

Lights slowly change – back to the room. ADEYEYE *gives* DAYO *a look. He nods back. The door opens,* KIERON *peeks through.*

KIERON. Still here? We gotta be out in ten, I ain't paying no overtime, so you / need to…

DAYO. I forgive you.

A confused KIERON *edges in. Beat.*

I had no older brother to help me… to lean on, punch, fight… hold. You didn't just block him out, you blocked me out too and I hated it… hated you, but… I still missed you. I want to start again… *we* can start again. I forgive you.

KIERON *starts to laugh. His laugh grows and grows… then stops.*

KIERON. Fuck your forgiveness.

A long beat. A stunned DAYO *starts off.*

DAYO. Blood ain't thicker than water. Not if you don't use the water to wash your eyes out and see the truth.

KIERON. FUCK YOUR TRUTH AND FUCK YOUR FORGIVNESS!!!

DAYO *stops.*

Kieron Owayale, national championships. Coach telling me, *You're destined, son! Destined for Gold!…* And it all turned to dust. Jumping from job to job, borrowing money from friends all to keep a roof over my head. Couldn't manage the bills, myself, let alone training!… Because of <u>him</u>. Do you know what that feels like? To have the one thing your soul ever wanted, snatched away from you, with no warning?! All because of his lie!

DAYO. It wasn't a lie, you pushed him!!

KIERON. There it is / right on time.

DAYO. He could hardly box / after it!

KIERON. You weren't even there.

DAYO. He was – he was / sure that you –

KIERON. Sure but not certain. But the whole family were certain that he was sure, so that was the story that stuck.

DAYO. I don't care about the story, I just want my brother back!

KIERON (*beat*). You had Mum, Dad.

DAYO. Dad was too busy playing happy families with his undercover one, and Mum?! Fed up, confused and depressed! And who could blame her?! Tryna hold two jobs, no support and then his sickle cell! She's a superhero, but she couldn't save us! So *I* carried the rest!

KIERON. What do you want me to say, thank you?!

DAYO. I wanted you to see beyond your pride!

KIERON. My pride is what kept me alive, kept me fighting!

DAYO. Life ain't a battlefield.

KIERON. It is when you're born with a knife in your hand.

DAYO. Why do you talk like that?! Like the world is constantly shooting bullets at you! We all lost something! He lost his boxing, I lost my freedom –

KIERON. I LOST MORE!!!

DAYO. According to who?!

KIERON. It's crazy 'cause today was about celebrating *his* life! Looking to the future! And you're here tryna drag us back! I tried, man, I tried, but there's certain things you just can't teach a man.

DAYO. I ain't one of your / students!

KIERON. Certain things are common sense, but that's the thing about common sense innit, ain't so common.

KIERON *starts off.*

DAYO. That's it. Run away again.

KIERON. WATCH YOUR MOUTH.

DAYO. Running and running and / running –

KIERON. I AIN'T RUNNING FROM NOTHING!

DAYO. Running and running and –

KIERON. I SWEAR DOWN YOU NEED / TO HOLD YOUR –

DAYO. RUNNING AND RUNNING AND WHAT IF HE WAS STILL ALIVE IF YOU HAD STOPPED!!!

KIERON *stops. Beat.*

What if you strengthened him, me, *us* and that strength gave him the hope he needed to push through, hold on, for longer… What if you staying changed the story and the outcome…

KIERON*'s back and shoulders tighten.* ADEYEYE *dips his hand in the water, runs over to* KIERON…

ADEYEYE. What if…

…*Gently touches* KIERON*'s back. His shoulders loosen slightly.*

KIERON. What if…

KIERON *seems conflicted, but then looks at the casket. Lights rise on it. He walks over, kneels down and tentatively dips his fingertips in, for a brief moment, then takes them out. As with* DAYO*, there is something distinctly different about the tone of the following. The words 'Why did he lie?' will be a voice-over, as if replaying the pervading question in his mind that he's asked himself his whole life.*

What *if* I picked up the phone? Opened the door? Put my hand out, rewrote the stories. You think those what-ifs ain't been playing inside my body all these years? Just put your hand out, man, put your hand out. But every minute, day, week that passed made my hand heavier, fist tighter, until letting go felt like letting my heart stop. So I kept replaying that moment, the day I left and all the choices I made after it, kept replaying the whys instead of the what-ifs – *why did he lie?* – asking myself and screaming out to the world – *why did he lie* – it was an accident, I brushed past him, I didn't know he was so close to the – *why did he lie* – Yeah, he got in touch, but it was a year after it happened, the damage was done! Takes thirty days to build a habit, a thought pattern, and I had a whole year to build a sea of them! And like an addict, even if you know that shit ain't good for you – *why did he lie?!* – even if you can *see* beyond the *sea* you're still stuck! – *why did he die?!* (*Beat.*) And leave me stuck?… Leave me split off from myself? And whenever I try and reach down to pick up the split-off parts, it's like I'm reaching down to pick up these small fragile crystals, wearing thick gloves, I just keep slipping through. So I stay scattered, I stick to <u>my</u> truth! Life ain't supposed to be easy! Shit happens! You do what you can to cope, to control, to keep your head above water, 'cause what other choice do I have?!… THERAPY?! (*Laughs.*) I mean, yeah, I've thought about it! I even rang them one time, when things got really… when the pillow knew my head more than I knew myself, but I couldn't – I… At first I thought it was pride. Pride, protecting honour, but… *Now, I see…* it was pride protecting a question… That silent question that lingers in my body, keeps me up at night, stops me dead in my tracks… Where do I start??? (*Beat.*) I did it! Booked and paid! Walk into the room, sit on the sofa, do the awkward introductions, take a sip of water and then what?? Tell me, where the *fuck* do I even start??? It's not talking to some stranger I'm afraid of, it's the starting. 'Cause the truth is, it wouldn't be with words… Truth is, I'd walk in and… I'd walk in and… and… and…

He bursts into a full bodied and silent roar.

(*Beat.*) Then flood every corner of that office with my tears. (*Beat.*) What therapist, in their right mind wants to deal with a screaming, crying, Black man. (*Beat.*) My whole life, no one's believed me, no one ever… So why would I let myself… open myself to a stranger? Ain't safe, man… The world ain't safe.

KIERON *stands from the casket.* DAYO *edges closer to* KIERON. ADEYEYE *begins to hum 'Amazing Grace' over…*

DAYO. We deserve peace!

KIERON. Oh, I've been waiting! Waiting for God to strike me down with that peace, been on my knees searching for it, like a man in the desert searching for –

DAYO. No one's perfect –

KIERON. I'm a father – a husband – a brother – a man of integrity – Honour – Strength – Resolve – I AM A BLACK MAN AND I'M SUPPOSED TO BE PERFECT! (*Beat.*) and if I'm not, it… it all crumbles… *I* crumble… and I can't… I…

ADEYEYE *steps closer to* KIERON, *hums louder.* KIERON *gazes at him.*

Why would it save a wretch like me? Why would it find *me*?! Nah, I'm not lost! Just gotta keep it together, keep it clean, 'cause if I keep it together and keep it clean – if I keep it – keep it – keep it –

KIERON *vigorously cleanses his body with his hands.* ADEYEYE *stops humming.* DAYO *tries to restrain* KIERON *as he spirals out of control, but to no avail.* DAYO *steps back, hopeless.* ADEYEYE *bolts forward…*

ADEYEYE. **I FORGIVE YOU!!!**

KIERON *stops, in shock. Beat.*

I forgive you. (*Beat.*) **Do you forgive me?… Do you forgive me?…**

KIERON *turns away… a brief yet conclusive inner conflict. Then, his body fully softens for the first time. He looks up and physically responds back: 'I forgive you.' Then extends his hand to his brothers…* ADEYEYE *moves towards the casket, ready to dip his hands in ritual preparation. But* DAYO *intercepts him: 'Not yet…' and diverts to retrieve the wooden box. He gives it to* KIERON, *who takes the box, hesitant. But he eventually opens it, to reveal…*

A bottle of Radox shower gel. He laughs.

DAYO. Now, you have to **forgive yourself**.

KIERON. No, not that. I… I can't – I don't deserve it, man, I deserve to –

DAYO. We deserve peace. We deserve peace. <u>We deserve peace.</u>

DAYO *and* ADEYEYE *begin the cleansing ritual.* KIERON *begins it, for the first time.*

KIERON. I deserve peace? (*Beat.*) <u>I deserve peace…</u>

DAYO. Let it wash over you…

ADEYEYE. **Cleanse you…**

KIERON. How?

DAYO. Surrender and let it –

KIERON. **Wash over me?**

ADEYEYE. **Cleanse you…**

DAYO *and* KIERON *riff off each other, grow around the space, each other, then, towards the casket.* ADEYEYE *steps back, in awe.*

KIERON. **Wash over me…**

DAYO. **Cleanse you…**

The above sequence builds and repeats multiple times, then crescendoes into DAYO *and* KIERON *simultaneously kneeling and plunging their hands into the casket. As soon as their hands enter, 'Give It to the Water' by Stormzy begins playing.*

KIERON *looks up and locks eyes with* ADEYEYE. *A shared moment of warmth passes between them.* ADEYEYE *joins them, kneeling to submerge his hands in the casket's waters.*

The brothers interlace fingers, lifting their connected hands with eyes closed. In unison, they begin the cleansing ritual, which swells into moments of them soulfully rubbing their bodies with the water. Rising to their feet, this sacred moment organically transforms into a collective physical odyssey of holds and lifts, tender yet charged. During this, there is a moment where KIERON *bursts out of the collective sequence and into an aggressive boxing motif. The brothers see him but don't approach because, with each punch, the aggression leaves his body, and with each punch, softness enters, until the punches become soft and flowing… like water.*

After a beat, the men reconnect through a final movement sequence, no longer estranged, no longer just brothers, but pillars supporting one another as they navigate the depths of collective grief and rediscovered love. The sequence crescendos and the brothers stand…

Connected. Empowered. Changed.

Epilogue

The brothers kneel in front of the casket. They collectively look out to the audience for a moment. The auditorium lights gently brighten. Their eyes meet each other, and they take a deep and meaningful breath in, and –

Exhale…

In… and –

Exhale…

In… and –

The swelling roar of the sea floods the space –

Exhale…

Lights fade on the brothers and in the auditorium –

Exhale…

The sound of the sea merges with their breath, its distant roar growing louder –

Exhale…

Darkness. The sea's primal rush now the only thing we hear, full and robust, it rushes –

Closer… Closer…

The waves sweep the theatre, wash the walls, swish under our feet, run towards us…

Closer… Closer…

The waves are about to wash right over us…

And…

they do.

The End.

A Nick Hern Book

Now, I See first published in Great Britain in 2024 as a paperback original by Nick Hern Books Limited, The Glasshouse, 49a Goldhawk Road, London W12 8QP, in association with Stratford East

Cover photography by Camilla Greenwell; cover design by Doug Kerr

Designed and typeset by Nick Hern Books, London
Printed in the UK by Mimeo Ltd, Huntingdon, Cambridgeshire PE29 6XX

A CIP catalogue record for this book is available from the British Library

ISBN 978 1 83904 363 5

Woodland CARBON
www.woodlandcarbon.co.uk
NICK HERN BOOKS
Printed on Carbon Captured paper

www.nickhernbooks.co.uk/environmental-policy